MW01659810

DEVIL IN A DIAPER

From Nightmare Infant to Son of My Dreams

ERIK LOHLA

ISBN: 0-9836785-1-0
ISBN-13: 978-0-9836785-1-9

www.devilinadiaper.com

To Preva,
The Best Wife In The World
(From Probably Only The Fifth
Best Husband)

And to Bentley Lohla, a.k.a. "Preva's Soulmate" (2004-2011):
Thank you for being such a
sweet, loving, and important
part of our lives.

You left us too soon.
We miss you too much.

Everything you are about to read is true.
Only the diapers have been changed to protect the innocent.

• • • • •

I can't help but feel a little bad as I write this. Because as I re-read the pages that follow, it kind of sounds as if I didn't like my newborn son.

There's a very good reason for that. I *didn't* like him. I didn't understand him. He made me crazier than a Trader Joe's parking lot.

Jack, like most newborns and like *all* newborns with colic, did everything he could to make our lives miserable. For the first three months of his life, he made us feel angry, depressed, exhausted, and worst of all, unappreciative, of the amazing life we have.

But even though I didn't like him, I still loved him.

I loved him with every fiber of my being, even during the hardest of nights. I would have died for him, and there were times, when my brain nearly simultaneously exploded in frustration and shut down from sheer fatigue, that I thought I might.

By the same token, I can't believe how many genuinely funny moments our baby-induced delirium created, especially in hindsight.

I wrote this book because I want other people to know that it's okay to feel whatever they feel when dealing with a newborn. I want them to know that even if they don't *like* their baby, it doesn't mean they don't *love* their baby. But most of all, I want them to know that it gets better.

Jack is now two years old. He's the cutest, sweetest, and funniest kid I've ever been around. He went from constantly crying to hardly ever crying. He now sleeps fourteen hours a night, except for the rare occasions when he only sleeps twelve.

The new Jack is even considerate. After we get out of the shower and he poops on the floor, he usually has the decency to say, "Uh-oh."

I'm glad that I have this record to help me remember. Otherwise, I might not fully recall what a whiny, nightmarish baby he was or what a whiny, sleep-deprived dad I was.

Back then, I just wanted to survive the day, and now I can't imagine my life without him. Because that's my son. That's my Jack.

• • • • •

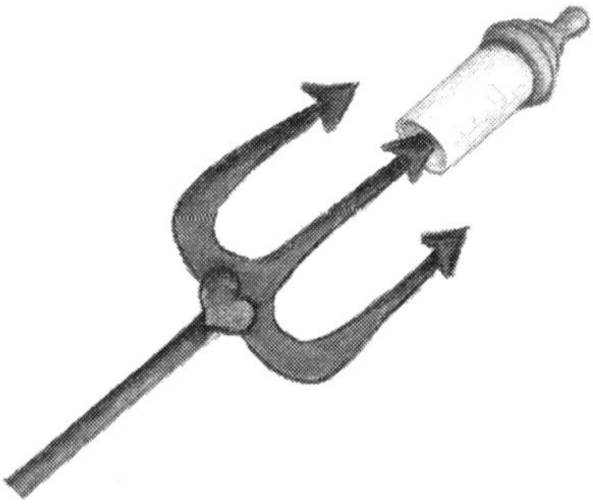

INTRODUCTION

I'm a good person. I'm a good father. *Why is he crying?* I work hard. I give to charity. *Why is he still crying?* One day, a puppy with no collar wandered into our garage. I spent the next twelve hours putting up fliers all over town trying to find its owner. He peed on our carpet, and when I picked him up because he was scared of our large dogs, he peed in my face. *Why won't he stop crying?* I washed the carpet, I washed the dog, and then I washed my face. While I was washing my face, he peed on the carpet again. *What's with the crying and will it ever stop?* At around midnight, I finally got a call and found out the dog belonged to a man who lived three houses away. We'd only lived in the neighborhood for two months, but I still felt stupid. *I don't have to know all the answers. I'm not even concerned with the meaning of life. I just want to know why he won't... stop... crying...*

It's 1:28 a.m. on October 7, 2009, and the son I've wanted my entire life is driving me insane.

I'm 37 years old and I've never been this frustrated or exhausted. But as frustrated and exhausted as I am, my prevailing emotion is fear. He's only ten days old, but he terrifies me.

When he's asleep, I'm scared that he's going to wake up. When he's awake, I'm scared that he's going to cry. When he starts crying, I'm scared that it will never stop. And more often than not, it doesn't until his little nine-pound body shuts down from sheer fatigue. But then, that nine-pound body is somehow recharged twenty minutes later.

It's a strange thing to be absolutely petrified of something that spends all day drinking, spitting up, and pooping, but I am. I spent two years living in a fraternity house with forty guys who did the same thing, but for some reason it was more funny than scary. Almost charming.

I'm not scared of crying. I'm scared of crying that has no cause and seemingly never ends. I'm scared that every time he opens his eyes, he's going to clench his fists and scream like a teenage girl who can't log onto her Facebook page.

My three-year-old daughter didn't cry until she got her vaccinations at two months old. My son might not stop crying *until* he's two months old, and based on the current state of affairs, I think I'm being optimistic.

I always thought that I could handle anything that a baby might throw at me… or throw up *on* me. But now I feel differently. Because as I lie here at 1:32 am, physically and emotionally drained, listening to the son I've always wanted scream like a child possessed, I'm wondering how exactly I'm going to get through this.

I'm not sure it's a good idea to write a book when you're getting four hours of sleep a night. For that matter, I'm not sure it's a good idea to drive a car or pee standing up on four hours of sleep. But when you have a newborn, you don't always have a choice.

My plan is to document my life and my rapidly deteriorating sanity over the next three months. That's how long most newborns, especially colicky ones, do everything they can to sabotage their parents' lives.

I have a feeling I'm about to experience something much different, much harder, and much more frustrating than anything I've ever experienced in my life. I don't want to burden anyone else with my problems, but... actually, I guess I do, or you wouldn't be reading this.

My hope is that writing this will be good for at least one of three things:

1) As a form of therapy to help me get through this.
2) As a journal to give support and maybe a few laughs to other parents who are going through (or who have gone through) this or anything remotely like it.
3) As a record of the events that led to my demise, in the event that I don't survive. In such case, to my beautiful wife and daughter, I leave everything. And to my newborn son, I don't leave jackshit. My son's name is Jack. The irony isn't lost on me.

October 7, 2009
10:22 am

I just told my wife Preva that I've decided to write a book. I think it went pretty well.

ME: "I'm writing a book about this."
PREVA: "Huh? Please get me a diaper. His jammies are soaked."
ME: "It's gonna be about..."

PREVA: "Diaper!"
I get a diaper and return ten seconds later.
ME: "Can I tell you about the book now?"
PREVA: "What? Oh, yeah. Book."
ME: "I'm writing about Jack and how crazy it is having a colicky baby. It'll be like a journal."
PREVA: "You mean a diary?"
ME: "No, a journal."
PREVA: "Twelve-year-old girls write diaries."
ME: "It's a journal. Maybe it'll turn into a book. This could be the craziest phase of our lives, so I thought it might be entertaining for other parents going through the same thing. If we survive, it might even be funny."
PREVA: "Are you serious?"
ME: "Yes."
PREVA: "You've gotta be kidding me. How are you gonna write a book?! You have an infant, a three-year-old, two jobs, four animals, a cranky wife who hates her body, and you're barely sleeping!"
ME: "Exactly! So, do I have your support?"
PREVA: "Whatever. Can you take Jack? I have to pump. My nipples are about to explode."

The happy family, blissfully unaware
of what we were in for.

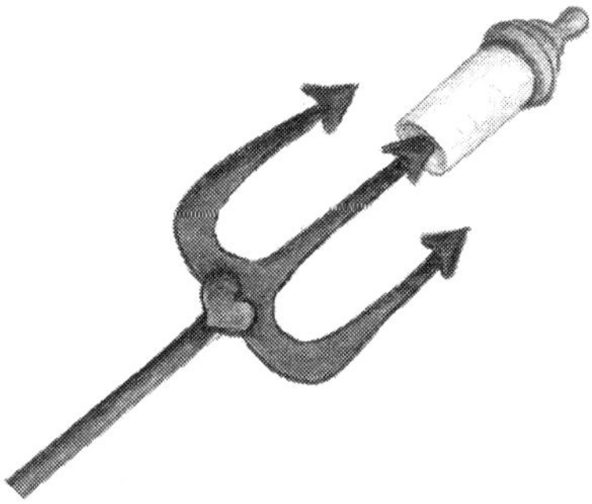

MONTH ONE

October 7, 2009
10:30 am

Jack Finn Lohla, the son I'd always wanted, was born Saturday, September 26, 2009. It was a beautiful, sunny fall morning when Jack entered the world, courtesy of a C-section and some wonderful mommy-calming medications. Ironically, it was his inability to cry that would give us our first cause for concern.

When he was born, he had fluid in his lungs that made him sound like a kid trying to suck the last few drops of juice out of a juice box. According to the doctor, if he had cried when he was born, it would have cleared the fluid. Preva and I exchanged a knowing smile. We weren't surprised. Our kids don't cry.

For the rest of the day, he was hooked up to various machines measuring various things and it was 50/50 whether he would have to be moved to another hospital with a NICU to monitor him overnight Eventually, the fluid cleared and the doctors said he'd be okay.

We were elated. And to us, Jack's refusal to cry during such an event could only mean one thing: he would be even easier and mellower than his sister.

Our three-year-old daughter Julia was a dream baby who ate when she was supposed to eat, slept when she was supposed to sleep, and pooped at times that were convenient and in amounts that we could handle. Naturally, we took credit for our dream baby, believing the love we gave her and the "schedule" we put her on were what made her so good. She fit into our lives happily and comfortably like Kirstie Alley in a Snuggie. There was no reason to think that our son would be any different.

The next few days were fine for Jack, but rough for mom. She could barely sit up, let alone walk to the bathroom on her own. With natural births, it's the actual birth that's hell. With C-sections, it's the next few weeks.

Amazingly, the nurses viewed helping Preva feed and change the baby as a favor rather than their job. They were slightly better about making sure she had her pain meds, except for the soft-spoken Asian nurse who tried to convince her that embracing Jesus was the best way to reduce the pain of the deep, six-inch incision on her stomach. As soon as Preva told her she was Jewish, it was goodbye Jesus, hello Vicodin.

Finally, we brought Jack home, ecstatic that he was healthy and content with the knowledge that we would have an effortless transition into the next phase of our lives as a happy, healthy, drama-free family of four.

For the first two nights at home, he was angel. He reminded us a lot of his sister, in both appearance and temperament. His sleep was sporadic, but each time he woke up, a mixture of affection and breast milk would quickly put him back to sleep. But on the seventh day, something changed.

For the next three days and nights, Jack went from a baby slowly getting used to the world to a baby who realized he hated the world. When he breathed, he grunted. When he drank his bottle, his head thrashed back and forth and his faced turned red. When he cried, he screamed and clenched his fists. And when he slept... well, he didn't really sleep.

We were confused. What had happened to our perfect child? What had we done wrong? Were we not feeding him enough? Were we feeding him too much? Was he allergic to our pets? Was he allergic to us? Nothing made sense, especially in light of our combined six hours of sleep.

Preva took Jack to the doctor to see if something might be wrong. She reported her disturbing findings to me that evening when I returned home from work.

"I have some bad news," she said.

"And you are who, exactly?" I replied, being too tired to make out human faces at that point. She said that her name was "Preva" and that she'd been my wife for the past five years. I nodded, the name vaguely ringing a bell.

"Dr. Yen thinks that Jack might have colic" she said.

"That's terrible. I don't believe this," I said. "By the way, what's 'colic'?"

"It's where a baby is always fussy and crying and there's no real cure for it," she said. "It starts when they're about a week old."

Her words sent shivers down my spine, because at exactly one week old is when Jack started needing an exorcist.

"Come on. There has to be *something* we can do," I pleaded.

"Some pediatricians think it's caused by gas, so Dr. Yen mentioned some new kind of formula and an herbal remedy called 'Gripe Water' that we can try," she said.

"But the odds are that we'll just have to wait until Jack grows out of it."

I found that to be about as soothing as airport toilet paper.

"He might not have colic," I reasoned. "He's really only been like this for three days. Maybe tonight will be different."

She nodded, more to appease me than because she agreed. But in the end, I was right. That night would be different. Not for him, but for me. I'd never had a night like that in my thirty-seven years on this earth.

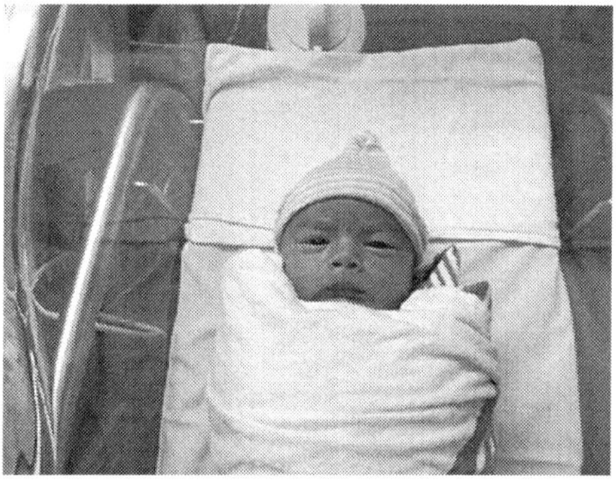

"Don't take my picture or I'll make the next three months of your life hell. Oops, too late. Sucks for you."

October 7, 2009
11:04 am

My recollection of the events of October 5th, 2009 are hazy, but that's probably for the best. Remembering too much would probably push me over the edge and further loosen my already fragile grasp on reality.

The past few nights since Jack's transformation had been a nightmare of inefficiency, with both of us staying awake most of the night and winding up totally exhausted the next day.

Thus, we decided that on this night, I would go to sleep and she would do the eleven o'clock feeding before trying to put Jack down. Then I, fresh off four hours of sleep would then do the next feeding and put him back down. It was a good plan. Unfortunately, babies don't like "plans."

I tried to go to sleep in the guest room around 10:00, but it didn't take. Jack's screaming and my worry over Preva's mental state saw to that. When I tried to help, she implored me to go to sleep. There was no point in both of us being awake, she said. I finally got to sleep around one o'clock.

Exactly 58 minutes later, my door flew open and Preva ran over to me, tears streaming down her cheeks. "I can't do this! I can't do this! I'm going crazy!" she said, her nerves frazzled by pain and lack of sleep.

"How much has he slept?" I asked.

"Zero! He doesn't sleep! He doesn't fucking sleep!" replied my delicate flower of a wife.

"Relax. It'll be okay," I said as I kissed her and made her lie down.

"I just need one hour," she said, collapsing on the bed.

She was so exhausted that she was asleep before I closed the door. Jack was another story.

I walked into our bedroom to find a creature that was more monster than baby. He was red-faced and screaming a blood-curdling scream that kept getting higher in pitch and more staccato in nature, as he'd fight for quick choppy breaths to force the sound out.

Knowing he wasn't close to sleepy-land, I took him out of his cradle and held him, rocking him back and forth in my arms. He kept crying. I laid him in bed with me and stroked his head. He kept crying. I gave him some formula. He kept crying. I put him in his electric swing with the soothing music and bird chirp sounds. He kept crying. I stuck a pacifier in his mouth, but he spit it out and just kept crying.

As he continued to thrash and grunt, I tried to recall why we thought having a second child was a good idea.

"One is like one. But two is like twenty," friends would say, dispensing one of those intentionally depressing nuggets of wisdom that makes parents feel better about how much their own lives suck.

It was now 4:30 am and Jack hadn't slept in more than twelve hours. Newborns aren't supposed to go that long without sleeping, but what else could I do?

Why wouldn't he fall asleep? Was he cold? Was he hot? Had he eaten too much at his last feeding? I had no idea. I tried everything in my pathetically small bag of tricks, but nothing worked.

I was so tired, my arms were shaking. I was so tired, my teeth hurt.

Two more hours passed. It was now 6:30 in the morning. He still hadn't slept for more than a couple of minutes, and if he had, I wasn't aware of it.

Never in my life had I been up that late. Not in college. Not in Amsterdam. Not when Preva got food poisoning on our first trip to Las Vegas and had to be taken by ambulance to a hospital after being wheeled through the casino on a gurney like someone who'd eaten a lethal dose of prime rib at the buffet. Not ever.

Jack finally fell asleep at 6:53 am.

Preva entered the bedroom exactly ten minutes later to find me staring up at the ceiling with a crazy half-smile on my face.

"Oh my god! What time is it?! What's going on?! Have you slept at all?!" she asked.

"Not a wink," I replied. "What are we gonna do?"

Preva walked over to the bed and kissed me on the forehead.

"I am so sorry. We'll get through this," she said.

"I don't see how," I replied. "In four hours, I have to write jokes about guys being kicked in the nuts."

"Just pretend it's Jack being kicked in the nuts," she said.

I smiled somewhat evilly at the thought. By the way, I don't sit around writing jokes about guys being kicked in the nuts just for the heck of it. I'm a writer on "America's Funniest Home Videos," so that kind of thing is part of the job description.

"You should call in sick today," she said.

"I can't. Jokes about dogs dragging their butts across the carpet don't write themselves, you know."

Preva kissed me again and I went into my office to sleep for two hours before I got up and drove to work.

October 7, 2009
8:34 pm

Well, that's about it. That's all the backstory you need to know about us, Jack, and why having kids is a terrible idea.

From now on, I'll be writing about our son and the events of our horrible lives as they're unfolding, right after they've unfolded, or maybe even before they unfold if extreme sleep deprivation gives you the ability to predict the future.

It'll be interesting to see how he progresses and just how successful he is in his evil plan to destroy the marriage of two people who love each other and until now, thought they could handle anything.

So, we'll see how this goes. If the baby blogs are correct, I'll be doing this for the next three months. Or maybe even the next three years. It doesn't really matter. I'm already nuts.

October 8, 2009
2:39 pm

Jack just peed on me for the first time. Got me really good. It was as wet as it was metaphorical.

The only good thing about it is that he obviously has a great sense of comic timing. He must have heard me telling Preva that I was writing a book about him.

If he could have, he would have guided his pee stream out the door, down the hall, into my office, and directly onto my laptop, ruining my book just a few pages into it.

I didn't mind the dousing. It's a rite of passage for any parent of a baby boy, and besides, I admired the force of his stream. He got my neck, chest, and right arm with a very powerful blast from a very small wiener.

When we saw the first ultrasound that showed he was a boy, our doctor said, "It's either a small penis or a large clitoris." I'm sure that's his standard "it's a boy" joke, but it was the best joke I'd ever heard, because hearing that I was going to have a boy was the best news I'd ever heard. Or so I thought.

I've heard from friends that baby boys fall into two categories: those who rarely pee when you're changing them and those who always pee when you're changing them. Naturally, Jack falls into the latter category.

If there's anything he can do to make our lives busier or more difficult, he does it. It wouldn't surprise me at all if he called us tonight in the middle of dinner to ask if we'd be interested in switching to DirecTV.

October 9, 2009
10:39 pm

Preva and I have a new schedule that shakes out like this. She does the majority of "Jack-watch" during the day, we switch off between eight and eleven p.m., and then I take over until two a.m., three a.m., or whenever he's finally ready to conk out. On good nights, Jack will sleep two hours before waking up, at which point Preva takes over.

I would love to feed him and put him down sooner, but like most colicky babies, his crazy time is at night. Between eight p.m. and two a.m., he cries and squirms nonstop.

I always thought that I was a night person. But I'm only a night person in the sense that I can watch Letterman without dozing off. I'm not the kind of night person that I can handle a nine-pound baby who constantly needs to be held while I'm standing up and walking around.

I go into the office at "America's Funniest Videos" two or three days a week. The other days, I write from home for both that and "The Mark and Brian Radio Program," which is where I met Preva.

If you live on the west coast, you've probably heard of Mark and Brian. If you don't, then you've probably heard of radio.

Until Jack joined us, I enjoyed working from home. But now, working from home means writing for at most ten minutes at a time before I have to either feed Jack, change him, or plug my ears to keep from having to listen to his shrill, ear-piercing cries.

At the moment, he's laying on the bed in my office, staring up at the ceiling with his familiar angry, "I'm going to scream any minute" look on his face. He's been calm for about ten minutes. From eight p.m. to two a.m., ten minutes is all he goes without crying.

And... is it starting?... Yes it is... There he goes. Just like clockwork. What the hell is he so angry about? Wonderful. Four more hours of this. For the rest of my life, I will never take being able to get in bed at nine o'clock and falling asleep whenever I want for granted again. I never knew how good I had it for so very long.

A night nurse couldn't be that expensive, could it?

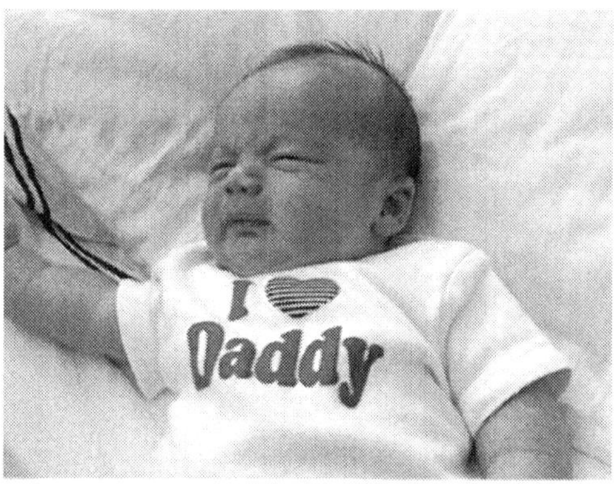

Could have fooled me.

October 10, 2009
11:53 pm

I've been standing up and holding Jack for exactly an hour. He just closed his eyes, so I put him back down on the bed. I keep thinking that one night, he'll go to sleep sometime before two a.m. for more than ten minutes at a time.

But as angry as Jack makes me, the show I was just watching pissed me off even more. I was flipping through the channels until I landed on one of those cable channels with "learning" or "discovery" in the title, which only has three types of shows: those featuring midgets, people with two hundred pound tumors, and moms with too many kids.

I especially like the shows featuring moms with too many kids, because it makes moms who have a lot of kids and can't *afford* to have a lot of kids think, "Hmm... maybe if I had even more kids, I could get my own TV show to help pay for all these kids."

The mom on the "moms with too many babies" show that I was watching had "sextuplets," which means she had six babies at one time. Sadly, they didn't call her "sextomom." Probably because it sounded too risque or like she enjoyed sexting, which could actually *lead* to pregnancy and might have in her case, I don't know.

At any rate, "sextomom" gave perhaps the worst words of advice that I can ever remember hearing. Her kids are now four. But she was recounting how difficult the first few years, and especially the first few months, were.

"But," she said, "If I could give any parents of newborns out there some advice, it would be 'Don't wish it away'."

"Don't wish it away"?! Hmm... How to respond to that? What phrase comes to mind? Oh, I know. It's "Shut the fuck up!"

You just know that she was wishing away nearly every second of every day. Who could blame her? For the most part, her life must have been a pee-soaked purgatory followed by a diaper-scented hell.

I'm not saying that you should wish anything away, but if you do because it's incredibly frustrating or difficult, you should be allowed to without feeling guilty, and I'm not going to let Sextomom make me feel guilty. At best, "Don't wish it away" is unrealistic, and at worst, it's patronizing.

Don't get me wrong. You shouldn't wish *all* of it away, just the part that's making you go batshit crazy. It's okay to wish away your baby crying so much that it makes your ears ring, or to wish away holding him so much that you sprain your neck, and for the entire next day, you can't look to your left. There are plenty of days where looking to my left is useful, even necessary.

I'm incredibly grateful that Jack's healthy, but I'll be so glad when this phase is over. I want my sanity back, I want my happy wife back, and I want my life back to the point where I don't wake up each day wishing that that day was over.

I'm doing my best to appreciate, remember, and document how cute Jack is when he's asleep, how adorably small he feels in my arms, and the brief moments that our eyes meet and I see the trust and love in his heart he has for me that he isn't even aware of yet.

But for now, I just want it to be over. Because this sucks.

October 11, 2009
12:10 am

Really, Jack? That's what you're going with? Good to know.

October 11, 2009
12:33 am

Tonight, while I was at the sink cleaning Jack's excrement from under my fingernails (which occurred when he had a crying fit right after I started changing his diaper), I realized that there might be a lot in this book about poop. A whole lot. There will also be bad language. Not a *&$#@*$ -load more, but a reasonable *&#$*@&% amount more nonetheless.

If you're offended, I really am sorry. But that's the way it is. If you're a parent, you understand. I have two cats, two dogs, a toddler, and a newborn, so my life pretty much revolves around poop.

The amazing thing is the way they stagger their movements. It's like the six of them have some sort of system to make sure that only one of them poops at a time in order to keep me as busy as possible.

Maybe they use something like Twitter. But instead of Twitter, it's "Shitter."

Shitter. Wow. I'm sorry about that, too. I'm just really tired. I'll end this right here. Besides, I have to go clean the litter box.

There are a lot of things in this house.
And they all poop.

October 11, 2009
2:03 am

I guess you should be careful what you wish for.

As amazing as Julia is, she's not a big cuddler. Even as an infant, she would practically push away if you tried to hold her. Preva wanted our next baby to crave affection and want to be held every second of the day. She got her wish.

Jack constantly wants to be held. He needs to be held. And we have to be standing up while we're holding him. It's the only thing that even somewhat soothes him.

Now, at the end of every day, our arms, our legs, our shoulders, and our backs ache like they've never ached before. Which makes me wonder... WHY THE HELL DO I HAVE TO BE STANDING UP?!

I don't get it. But more than intriguing than why I have to be standing up is how he knows when I'm standing up.

He's only thirteen days old and he can barely see, but he's clearly a genius, because he always knows where he is in relation to the ground. The instant I sit -- even though I hold him in the exact same way and with the exact same baby-soothing, arm-bobbing motion -- he starts screaming!

I realize Jack's not alone when it comes to this. I've heard from many people that their babies simply won't stand for sitting, so to speak. It must be something that's been in babies' DNA for millions of years ever since the cavemen had to soothe their cavebabies.

As bad as we have it, cavemen had it worse. They didn't have pacifiers, mobiles, or battery-powered swings. I think it's possible that the wheel was actually invented so that sleep-deprived cavemen could drive around their cranky cavebabies as a last resort.

On the plus side, when frustration reached its peak, they could just set the cavebabies outside the cave for a minute and a hungry woolly mammoth would take their problem off of their hands.

"Where's Gluk-Gluk?" the cave-husband would say in cave-speak to his cave-wife.

"I don't know, honey. I just turned my hairy, hunched back for a second and he was gone," the exasperated cave-wife with eight other cave-children would say.

"Sometimes I wish I'd never clubbed you over the head and forced myself on you," the cave-husband would retort.

"Well, maybe if you'd spend more time at cave and less time out trying to invent fire with your friends this wouldn't have happened," the cave-wife would respond.

Speaking of fire, there's a beautiful antique mahogany rocking chair in Jack's room, which used to belong to

Preva's grandmother. Every time I look at it, I feel like chopping it up and turning it into beautiful antique mahogany firewood, because that's the only thing I can see us using it for.

Julia's first word was "light," my first word was "Batman," and Preva's first word was "Mama."

I'll bet Jack's first words will be, "I loved jerking you around with the whole 'have to be standing up' thing. Man, that never got old. Good times. By the way, I just took a big dump, so you might want to take care of that."

October 11, 2009
9:52 am

Nordstrom is not only about the nicest department store you'll find, it also has the best return policy.

I really wish that Preva had gone into labor and birthed Jack inside of a Nordstrom. Because I think that, technically, they would have to take him back.

October 11, 2009
4:38 pm

This is one of those days when I'm grateful that I work from home and that I have such a caring and understanding wife.

She doesn't need as much sleep as I do and she knows that I need to average eight hours a night or I get colicky myself. There's no way to get eight hours these days, so I nap when I can. Never for very long. But every little bit helps.

A little before noon, I was trying to feed Jack in my office when he spit out the nipple and started crying. He then arched his back so suddenly and violently that I nearly dropped him.

I was so scared and upset with myself for nearly dropping him that I threw his bottle through the open door into the hallway before yelling an especially satisfying string of expletives.

It was long and, grammatically, it didn't make sense, but it felt good. Seconds later, I saw an out-of-breath Preva in the doorway. She had abruptly stopped pumping and was covering her breasts with two red plastic party cups.

"Is everything alright?" she asked.

"I think so," I said, staring into space.

"Honey, why don't you take a nap?" she asked, looking concerned.

"I'm fine."

"You're not fine. You just threw Jack's bottle down the hall. Please take a nap," she pleaded.

"No, you have to pump. I'm good," I said, not feeling anywhere close to good.

"You scared Snort," she said, referring to one of our two pit bull mixes. It's amazing that two dogs who can be so intimidating can also act like the biggest wimps in the history of dogs, let alone pit bull mixes. I named him Snort, because, well, that's what he does.

"He's in the bathroom, shaking," Preva added.

Every bad boy has a soft side.

"Maybe a nap would be good," I said.

She nodded as I handed her Jack. She wasn't happy that I couldn't give her twenty minutes to pump, but she also knew that I'd reached my limit of what I could handle. I think that's the sign of a good marriage -- knowing when the other person has reached the limit of what he or she can handle. I'm glad we have a good marriage. I don't know how people can do this who don't.

"Are you going to write about this?" she asked.

"Probably. Why?"

"If you do, please don't write that I was covering my boobs with two big red party cups," she said.

"Don't worry. I'll say it was a towel or something."

"Thanks. Enjoy your nap, baby."

Like I said, we have a good marriage. I know what I can get away with and she knows that two big red party cups just makes a better story.

October 11, 2009
7:58 pm

I just read on the Internet that it's estimated that anywhere from ten to forty percent of babies have varying degrees of colic. It also said that most doctors don't even bother diagnosing colic, because there's rarely anything that can be done about it.

It's truly one of the great medical mysteries. But what's certain is that the millions of parents who've had a colicky newborn will probably never experience anything as frustrating or exhausting.

The crazy thing about many of these parents who are nearly driven crazy is that they don't even know their baby has colic. All they know is that their baby cries a lot, can rarely be soothed, and that the screaming fits are usually worse at night – often from seven or eight p.m. until sometime after midnight.

I'm 37 years old, already have a three-year-old child, and I didn't know what "colic" was or that a baby could actually be like this. I wish I still didn't.

October 12, 2009
1:08 am

Feeding Jack is like one of those bad action shows where the hero has to disarm a bomb by cutting either the blue wire or the red wire. He stares at them until the countdown timer nears zero, snips a wire, and holds his breath. He always cuts the correct wire, because the stars of action shows rarely blow themselves up.

When I'm about to feed Jack, I have to make sure everything is just right: the temperature of the bottle, the formula-to-water ratio, and the angle of his neck. He won't eat if it's too quiet. He won't eat if it's too loud. He won't eat if he's naked. He won't eat if he's just a little hungry, nor will he eat if he's starving. If each and every condition isn't met, my baby bomb explodes. He spits out every drop of the initial sip and immediately starts crying.

That requires an outfit change (always his and sometimes mine), a diagnosis of where and how the feeding went wrong, and for me to calm him down enough to eat, all of which takes about thirty minutes.

TV show bombs only have two wires, but my baby bomb has about twenty wires. When there are two wires, you have a 50% chance of snipping the right wire, but when there are twenty wires, you only have a 5% chance of not screwing it up. With Jack, I hardly ever snip the right wire and my baby bomb explodes.

The good news, I don't die. The bad news, I want to.

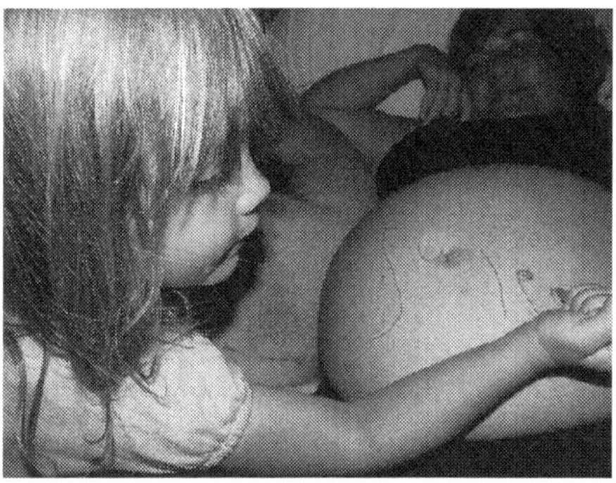

In war, soldiers write messages on the bombs they drop on the enemy. Here's Julia writing on the one about to explode on us.

October 12, 2009
4:35 pm

Today, Preva and I were struck with a rather disturbing thought. What if Jack doesn't have colic? What if he's just a really big wussy?

"Really Big Wussy" isn't a clinical term, as far as I know, but it describes Jack to a tee. Absolutely everything bothers him. When you dress him, he cries. When you put him down, he cries. When he's eating, he cries. When you talk to him, he cries.

The signs of colic include "extreme irritability," but not even that broad definition seems to do Jack justice. What if it's not colic? What if he never grows out of it? What if this is just who he is?

Yesterday, Preva called our doctor:

DR. YEN: "Is he eating?"
PREVA: "Yes."
DR. YEN: "Sleeping?"
PREVA: "Yes."
DR. YEN: "Having regular movements?"
PREVA: "Everyone but me, yes."
DR. YEN: "As I said, it sounds like he might be a bit colicky. Did you try the Gripe Water?"
PREVA: "Yeah, it didn't work."
DR. YEN: "Sorry. But it seems to help some babies, so it was worth a shot."

"Gripe Water" is a home remedy that contains things like ginger, fennel, and chamomile and is supposed to help with colic, gastrointestinal problems, and other ailments.

It's based on the theory that colic is caused by gas. But just like the theories that an asteroid wiped out the dinosaurs or that tennis elbow killed Bigfoot, it's just a theory.

If you've had a cranky or colicky baby, you've no doubt been told by someone to try Gripe Water. We were told and we tried it for several days, following the recommended dosage instructions.

Unfortunately, it's been our experience that it hasn't improved our experience. That's not to say it won't help you. Just don't be surprised if it doesn't.

We've also had days where we've only given Jack breast milk and days where we've only given him formula. Jack's the same no matter what.

His crying isn't worse before he eats. It isn't worse after. It isn't worse before he poops or farts. It isn't worse after. It isn't worse before I burp him. It isn't worse after.

Some colic might be caused by gas or stomach discomfort. Jack's isn't.

Because of that, this is how Preva *hoped* the conversation would go:

DR. YEN: "Is he eating?"
PREVA: "Yes. He's also sleeping, peeing, and pooping. Sometimes all at once. The thing is, he's just a really big pain in the ass."
DR. YEN: "It sounds like he's a bit colicky, but it's nothing to worry about."
PREVA: "Is there anything we can do? Is there someplace we might be able to send him for a few months?"
DR. YEN: "Have you tried Gripe Water?"
PREVA: "Ha! Gripe Water?! Is that all you've got?! That's 'page one' of 'Colicky Babies For Dummies' and just for the record, it doesn't do squat."

DR. YEN: (LAUGHING) "I know it doesn't. That's just a little joke among us pediatricians. The truth is, nothing works. But it would be hard to justify twelve years of medical school if we didn't tell parents something, right?"
PREVA: "That's true. Anyway, doctor, we were wondering if it's possible that Jack's just a really big wussy."
DR. YEN: "Is your husband a really big wussy?"
PREVA: "He can be. Especially when he's sick or watching sports."
Dr. Yen: "Interesting. Is this a secure line?"
PREVA: "Huh?"
DR. YEN: (WHISPERING) "Please bring Jack in as soon as you can. I'll need to run a few tests."
PREVA: "What kind of tests?"
DR. YEN: "Scientists at UCLA recently identified the "Really Big Wussy Gene" and I'd like to see if Jack has it. If he does, and it's alright with you, they could even name it after him."
PREVA: "They could call it the 'Jack gene'."
DR. YEN: "Has a nice ring to it, doesn't it?"
PREVA: (SOBBING) "I suppose."
DR. YEN: "Oh, one more thing. Nothing we do for him will be covered by your health insurance."

October 13, 2009
12:39 am

Tonight, something happened with Jack that gave me a bit of hope. We were giving him a bath in the bathroom sink and naturally, he was crying the entire time. Preva was getting tense and I was, too. Baths soothe most babies, but not Jack.

While I was holding him so that Preva could soap his body, I noticed that I was emitting an interesting odor myself. Between working and watching Jack nonstop, I'd forgotten that I hadn't showered in two days until my underarms kindly reminded me.

But then, as if struck by divine perspiration, I grabbed Jack and took him in the shower with me.

As soon as the water hit his head and started cascading down his body, he stopped crying. He started breathing normally. His body relaxed and he started looking around calmly and thoughtfully as if a new, happier, more emotionally satisfying world had just opened up to him.

Preva and I were speechless. We'd literally never seen this side of him before. He didn't care when water got in his eyes or that -- because I was so afraid of dropping him -- I squeezed him tight enough to make poop shoot out of his butt with such force that it could shatter the shower door.

I love showers, so perhaps Jack does, too. Maybe while we were in there, he started looking inward and meditated on how his irrational and frustrating behavior really isn't benefitting anyone. Maybe it brought him peace because the water's warmth reminded him of being in the womb. Or maybe it just felt good on his balls.

For whatever reason, he loved it. I soaped him up, rinsed him off, and handed him back to Preva who wrapped him in a towel. We held our collective breath. Jack, however, didn't hold his and let it out in the form of his usual obnoxious, incredibly disconcerting cry.

Jack loved his shower, but sadly, there was no residual effect. Preva got him dressed while I stayed in the shower until the water got cold.

PHOTO DELETED DUE TO PALE,
OUT-OF-SHAPE-DAD

Jack and myself in the shower.

October 13, 2009
7:39 pm

Today, I was so tired that I nearly fell asleep while learning over to tie my shoes.

October 14, 2009
1:41 am

I always used to laugh to myself when I heard other parents say that they had to drive their babies around to get them to sleep. I fully remember wondering, "Why the heck don't they have their kid on a schedule?" in between chuckles. Well, I'm not laughing anymore. But I am so tired that I'm nearly hysterical.

Tonight, there was no other way to calm Jack down or to silence the blood-curdling screams that threatened to wake up other the family members who, unlike Jack, realize that there's -- to borrow an overused sports expression -- no "i" in "team."

However, there is an "i" in "colic," which is probably why Jack's sole purpose in life seems to be inconveniencing the rest of us. By way, there are also three "i's" in "inconveniencing." (In my current state, I had to count them about five times just to make sure.)

I never thought I'd turn into one of those dads who had to drive his baby around to get him to fall asleep. I feel like a failure. I feel like a cliché. I feel like a character on a sitcom that just got canceled. Julia's three years old and we never even had to think about doing that with her.

Still, I can't take for granted the fact that after about ten minutes of screaming in the car, Jack finally conked out. And apparently it was a deep sleep, because now that he's home and in his cradle, it looks like he's staying asleep.

It can't be good to hit the open road when I'm this tired, this frustrated, and I'll be honest, this angry. I made sure that I was awake enough not to fall asleep behind the wheel, but at the same time, my reaction time couldn't have been the sharpest it's ever been.

I don't want to make this a habit, but for now it seems to make sense. And for as long as I do, I'll make sure that I obey the speed limit, use my turn signal, and not talk on my cell phone. Because the last thing I want to do is get pulled over for a DWI (Driving With an Infant)*.

Even though it wasn't that bad and Jack did pass out from sheer exhaustion, I'm still hoping that I don't have to do this again for a while.

* Lame joke due to exhaustion**

** Exhaustion due to Jack***

*** Jack due to our belief that a second child was a good idea.

October 15, 2009
1:23 am

Shit. I had to drive Jack around again tonight. I can't let this become a habit. I lost to my 26-day-old son *again*.

For any of you "fantasy baseball" players out there, who might be thinking about joining a "fantasy infant" league (but really, why would you?), here's your score: Jack-2, Dad-0. That means that Jack would be a sold first round pick, while I would go undrafted.

But just like last night, I was simply too exhausted to hold and "shush" and tote him around in the Baby Bjorn until my knees ache and my back nearly gives out.

I loaded Jack into the car for another late night drive through Valencia.

In the car, I barely notice Jack's crying. It's white noise as I drive the quiet streets, wondering how many other parents are doing the same thing as I.

But as curious as I am, somehow I don't think that pulling up alongside another car, rolling down my window, and yelling, "Hey, you got a baby in there?!" would be either smart or worth the effort.

If there are other parents doing the same thing, I wonder how many of them have baby boys. I wonder how many are named Jack. I wonder how many parents find it interesting that on the 5 Freeway, there are two adjoining businesses with signs reading "Teague Custom Marine" and "Howard Custom Boats." Probably none. But I do.

"Teague" and "Howard" are the last names of two basketball players who played at Wake Forest and are now in the NBA. It's a coincidence, and a meaningless one at that, but one that made me laugh nonetheless. Because even though I'd seen the two signs hundreds of times before, this was the first time I'd made that connection.

It made me realize that I've spent way too much time watching sports. But it was comforting to know that in spite of my sleep deprivation, I can still amuse myself and perhaps others since I haven't been fired from either of my comedy writing jobs yet.

It also made me feel like it wasn't unsafe for me to be driving around the son whom I'm 72% sure I'll grow to love one day.

I have to remember that he's not just my son. In time, he'll also be my best friend. When that hits me, it makes everything just a little bit easier.

From now on, whenever I watch Josh Howard or Jeff Teague play basketball, I'll think of this night. And I'll smile, thinking that in another thirty years, perhaps Jack will be driving around his newborn and noticing signage that will make him remember when his own life was simpler and he had nothing better to do than sit on the couch and watch basketball.

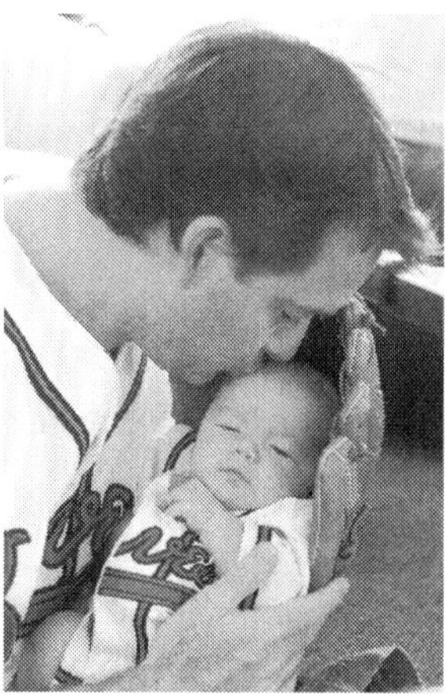

Hope you like sports. No pressure, though.

October 15, 2009
2:26 am

Is there a difference between spit-up and vomit? If not, "spit-up" doesn't sound as gross.

I'll just tell myself that that's what was caked on the jammies I was too tired to change Jack out of before putting him to bed.

October 16, 2009
7:58 am

This morning is a good reminder that Jack doesn't just cry at night. It's just worse at night.

I just got back from a ten-minute trip to Starbucks with Jack and he was crying so loud that my ears are ringing. I know that I'm typing because I can see my fingers moving. I just can't hear them tapping the keyboard.

We should have known that Jack would be like this. There were warning signs.

When Preva was pregnant with Julia, she hardly felt any kicking. Sure, she was always tired and uncomfortable, but it was nothing like it was with Jack. Jack was constantly tossing, turning, and kicking -- and it was always worse at night.

And then there was the trip to Hawaii. Or what was supposed to be the trip to Hawaii. I'm too tired to write about it now, but once I'm fully caffeinated I will. It explains a lot. Maybe everything.

October 16, 2009
1:50 pm

We thought a trip to Hawaii would be a good idea. One last fling before our second child arrived and such trips would become infinitely more difficult.

We drove to the airport, where a one-hour delay quickly turned into a six-hour delay. Apparently, there was a problem with the airplane's air conditioning system.

If there's one thing that a large, sweaty, uncomfortable pregnant woman doesn't want to hear before she gets on a plane, it's that there's a problem, which could cause her to become even sweatier and more uncomfortable.

My wife isn't a huge fan of flying even when the plane's on time and she's *not* carrying an extra forty pounds on her petite, four-foot-eleven frame (sorry, honey, I meant to write "five-foot-two frame").

As we walked toward the gate, we might have looked like a happily married couple flying to Kauai, but we felt like two prisoners headed to the electric chair -- a slim man of average height and a short woman nearly as wide as she was tall. From behind, we must have looked like the number "10."

Against our better judgment, we handed the flight attendant our boarding passes and headed down the ramp. By this time, Preva was taking deep breaths, exhaling so strongly she might have been able to cool down the entire plane with her breath in case the air conditioning system crapped out again. The only problem was that she had hot, angry, nervous breath, which would have only made the cabin warmer.

We stepped onto the plane and found our seats, which happened to be in an exit row. That meant more legroom.

It also meant the seats didn't recline. When my big, uncomfortable, pregnant wife who had been sitting at the airport for the past seven hours realized that her seat didn't recline, well, that's when things took a turn for the worse.

"Don't worry, honey," I said. "We'll figure something out."

"I don't believe this. I do not believe this. This is not happening." she replied in a rapid-fire monotone.

"It's gonna be okay," I said.

"Erik, I'm gonna freak the fuck out!"

"Just be patient," I said. "Can you please be patient? Will you please do that for me?"

"Yes," she nodded, taking several quick, hot breaths. I looked around for a stewardess to either find us new seats or shoot me in the head to put me out of my misery. There weren't any within view, so I turned around and addressed my fellow passengers.

"My wife is very pregnant and can't sit in an exit row, because her seat doesn't recline. Would anyone be kind enough to change seats with us?"

I asked as politely as I possibly could, and the thirty or so passengers who heard my plea just as politely went back to reading their magazines and checking their Blackberries.

I finally spotted a flight attendant, who seemed sympathetic to our plight. While she started to ask other passengers if they'd be willing to change seats with us, a friendly, twenty-something guy from the rear of the plane approached me.

"I'm with my wife and we're part of a big group traveling to Hawaii. My wife's in the bathroom, but she'll totally understand and switch with you guys," he told me.

"That's awesome. I can't thank you enough," I said, shaking our savior's hand before he headed back toward his seat. I exhaled and sat down next to Preva and told her that either this guy would come through or the flight attendant would find the two people on the plane who weren't assholes.

"Why are people such jerks? I would totally change seats with a pregnant woman," Preva said.

"I would, too," I replied, knowing in my heart that I truly would.

I believe that people are generally good, but this was one of the few times in my life where I've felt genuine disappointment in my fellow man.

I just should have realized that a "fellow man" flying to Hawaii to drink and sunbathe is probably more selfish than a "fellow man" flying to, say, Africa to build an orphanage.

Just then, the stewardess returned and said that nobody was willing to change seats.

"Can't you *make* them change seats?" I asked.

"Unfortunately, I can't," she said unsympathetically. "Is she going to be alright?"

"If you cared, you'd find someone to change seats with us," I replied.

I was steaming. I wanted to suffocate every person on the plane with one of those tiny airplane pillows, but that would take forever if it was even possible. Preva was nearly hysterical.

"It's alright," I said, trying to calm her down. "That guy from the back said his wife would change seats with us."

Just then, that guy from the back returned. From the look on his face, I knew that he didn't have good news.

"Sorry, but my wife doesn't want to switch seats," he informed us, expertly avoiding eye contact.

"But you said she'd understand," I said.

"She does."

"Just not enough to change seats, I guess."

He simply shrugged.

"You said you were with a big group of people, right? Will any of them change seats?" I begged.

"Yeah, no."

"'Yeah, no?' What do you mean, 'Yeah, no'? What's 'yeah, no'?" I asked, knowing full well what "yeah, no" meant. I was just annoyed. I hate it when people say, "Yeah, no" and I really hated it now.

"They don't want to change seats, either. I'm really sorry," he said.

I nodded as he returned to seat. His reclining, comfortable, perfect for a pregnant woman seat.

"Let's just get off the plane. We can still get off," I said.

"No, we're flying to Hawaii. We need this trip. I'll be fine," Preva replied, suddenly appearing calmer.

"Are you sure?" I asked, far from convinced.

She nodded and took a deep breath as she fastened her seatbelt. We started taxiing. I couldn't believe we were still on the plane. I was pretty sure we shouldn't be.

Preva's eyes were closed and she was taking deep breaths, mentally psyching herself up. I reached over to hold her hand. She squeezed my hand tighter than Popeye trying to open a can of spinach. We continued taxiing until we got to the runway to await our turn for takeoff.

"You okay?" I asked.

She nodded.

"We're going to laugh about this later," I said, trying to coax a smile.

"I know," she said, smile coaxed.

A few moments later, the pilot told the flight attendants to "prepare for crosscheck," whatever the hell that means.

We heard the engines start to rev and then we started down the runway, quickly gathering speed. I looked at Preva. She looked back. "I can't do this," she said.

"Huh? What? Are you kidding?" I asked.

She shook her head, her face turning paler by the nanosecond.

"What do you mean you can't do this? You're doing this! The plane's moving!" I said.

"I have to get off," she replied with a calmness that frightened me. "Do you understand? I have to get off. Now, Erik. Now."

I had two options. The first was having every passenger on the plane watch me tell a member of the flight crew that my wife was going to "freak the fuck out" if they didn't stop the plane. The second was ignoring my wife and having her actually freak the fuck out somewhere over the Pacific Ocean. This was by far the worse option.

I unclasped my seatbelt and quickly ran up the aisle until I found a seat belted male steward. Probably because of the panicked look on my face, he didn't ask me to return to my seat. He just weakly said, "Yes?"

"My wife needs to get off the plane," I calmly said.

"Are you sure?" he stammered, his eyebrows forming a teepee.

"Yes."

Realizing that I meant business, he simply said, "Okay," and sprung to action. Just as I did, he knew that it was better that this happened now rather than later. As I returned to my seat, I could feel the other passengers staring at me, but I didn't dare meet their gaze.

I sat back down, as the realization of what I had just done quickly set in. I had just stopped a plane.

My dad flew in the Navy. He was an amazing pilot who finished second in his flight class of 147 and landed on aircraft carriers. All I was capable of doing was stopping a plane that I wasn't supposed to stop.

Preva looked at me. "I'm so sorry," she said.

"I know," I said, holding her hand. My heart was racing and my face felt flush. My cheeks hadn't felt so red and hot since the time I accidentally peed my pants in fourth grade due to uncontrollable laughter from an impromptu game of "chalkboard eraser baseball" when the teacher was out of the room.

What were we thinking? Why had we even tried this? It was my fault. I wasn't the pregnant one, with my hormones all out of whack. I should have known better. Just then, the pilot came over the loudspeaker.

"Ladies and gentlemen, this is the pilot speaking. We have a situation with one of our passengers. We're gonna be turning the plane around and heading back to the gate. I'll give you more information after the passengers exit the plane. I apologize for the added delay, but we'll have you on the way to Kauai just as soon as possible."

I wish he would have just kept talking until we returned to the gate. Because when he stopped, the silence was deafening.

We both slunk lower in our seats, wishing we could close our eyes and magically disappear. A woman in the row ahead of us turned around and said, "It's okay. It's just a flight. You do what you need to do."

"Thank you," Preva replied, grateful for the support. I was, too. But if she was so sympathetic, why the hell didn't she and her husband switch seats with us?

We finally got back to the gate. The steward motioned to us and we started down the aisle, as every passenger on the plane glared at us. I was worried that someone might yell something rude.

But then it hit me: Why were we worried? If someone had switched seats with us, this wouldn't have happened. Up until Preva realized that her seat didn't recline, she was okay. This was just as much their fault as ours. I started *hoping* that someone would say something.

I began walking more slowly as I imagined the exchange in my mind:

MALE PASSENGER: "We've already waited six hours! If she's too nervous to fly, you shouldn't have even gotten on the plane!"
ME: "Listen, dickhead! If you'd switched seats with us, you'd be in Hawaii an hour sooner!"

We were on a plane full of moms, so even in the midst of the insanity, this is the exchange I imagined taking place in Preva's head:

FEMALE PASSENGER: "That is the cutest maternity shirt ever! Where'd you get it?!"
PREVA: "Aww, thank you! You don't think it's too blousy?"
FEMALE PASSENGER: "Not at all! It's super cute!"
PREVA: "I love you!"

We exited the plane and practically ran up the ramp toward the terminal. Preva started crying, as all of her feelings of fear, embarrassment, and frustration exited her body.

We collapsed in a heap on the floor, barely believing what we'd just done.

Preva started feeling cramping pains in her stomach that had both of us worried. I was going to call her doctor if it continued much longer.

But in the meantime, I did what I thought made sense. We walked to an airport restaurant and ordered a beer and a glass of wine.

Some doctors believe that it's okay for prego's to enjoy the occasional glass of wine. Preva never drank during her two pregnancies, but considering the circumstances, we felt it wasn't just "okay," but the smart thing to do. She hid the glass of Pinot under the table, taking the occasional sip, as her anxiety and stomach pains slowly went away.

We continued drinking as we alternately laughed and cringed while recalling the events of the past hour. If Julia Roberts was the "Runaway Bride," then Preva was the "Runway Bride."

There would be no trip to Hawaii. Jack saw to that. But that wouldn't be the last plan he ruined.

"Uh... sorry, I guess?"

October 16, 2009
11:31 pm

Tonight, my mom called. Before I even said, "Hello?" I asked her a question that I've been meaning to ask her ever since Julia was born: "Why the hell didn't you tell me that having kids was so hard?!"

I expected her to laugh or jokingly apologize or give me the kind of sympathy that no parent of a newborn can ever get enough of.

But instead, she simply said, "You forget."

I was struck by the simplicity and honesty of her answer. She never tried to tell me exactly what being the parent of a newborn was like, because she didn't *remember* exactly what being the parent of a newborn was like. Somehow, the years slowly erase all of the unpleasant recollections and replace them with happy family memories.

I could understand how my mom could forget, I told her. Except for one thing. I would never ever until the day I died -- and maybe not even after that -- forget how hard this is.

I told her it's Preva's theory that it's a conspiracy among all parents not to tell their children how difficult raising, or "rearing" as my dad would tell me, kids is. Otherwise, their kids might not have children and they wouldn't get to be grandparents. My mom laughed. But then again, she didn't try to debunk my theory.

My mom then told me about a conversation she'd recently had with her neighbor, who was also a grandmother. My mom mentioned to the woman that her grandson currently had colic. The woman proceeded to tell my mom that she had had five children, the last of whom had colic.

She said that this fifth baby was more difficult than all of her other four babies combined. She would have rather gotten pregnant, felt fat for nine months, gone through the pain of giving birth, and dealt with the rigors of taking care of a newborn four more times than endure what her colicky daughter put her through.

It was then that she said that she, unlike my own "motherhood was never difficult for me" mother, would never forget how difficult it was having a baby like that. I smiled and felt an instant connection with this 70-year-old, San Diego-dwelling grandmother whom I'd never met.

I felt her pain and I would imagine that to some degree, she's feeling mine. Because we're both members of a club which nobody wants to join and which everybody wants to be kicked out of as soon as humanly possible.

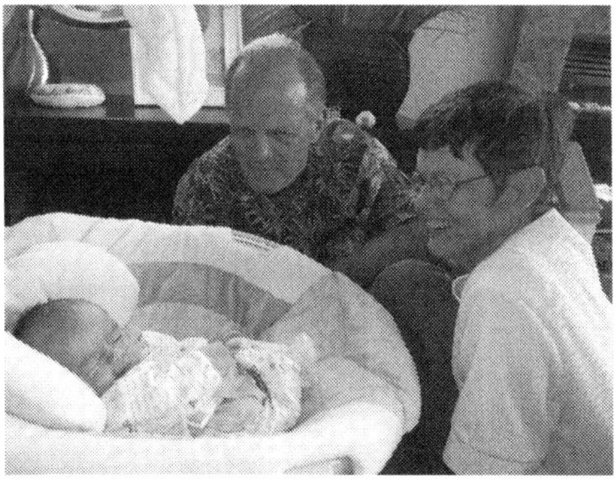

MY MOM: I told Erik that we forgot how difficult being a parent is.
MY DAD: Did he fall for it?
MY MOM: Seemed to.
MY DAD: (wringing hands evilly) Excellent.

October 17, 2009
12:01 am

Nearly every parent I talk to says that their son is whinier than their daughter.

And nearly every wife I talk to says that their husband is whinier than their child.

If males are indeed whinier when they're tired or sick, I have a theory that I believe explains it. You see, ladies, most of us have the skin around our penis removed or "circumcised" when we're born.

From what I've seen and experienced, this hurts quite a bit. And yes, we cry a lot as a result. But I don't think the amount of crying is quite equal to the amount of physical and psychological trauma that we endure. We still have more to crying or, as you might call it "bitching," to do. We simply choose to do this slowly and gradually over the course of our entire lifetimes.

Thus, what you view as your husband's or son's whining, complaining, or inability to handle pain is simply residual whimpering left over from our circumcisions. It's science. Deal with it.

October 17, 2009
2:57 am

Fuck!

October 17, 2009
8:03 am

When we realized that Jack had colic, I thought that I would have trouble falling asleep at night. I thought that I would be so worried that he might start crying at any minute that it would prevent me from falling asleep. In reality, I've never fallen asleep more quickly than I have over these past two weeks.

By the time two a.m. finally arrives, my body and mind are so exhausted that I pass out two seconds after my head hits the pillow. But last night was different.

Last night, I struggled to fall asleep as I worried about my son. It was irrational worry about who he was and what he would become, but it was worry nonetheless. I can't shake the thought that, what if it's not colic? What if this is just who he is?

At three years old, we already know that Julia has the confidence and smarts to handle whatever life throws at her. She has the best parts of Preva and the best parts of me. But Preva has more best parts than I do, which means that Julia has more Preva than Erik in her, and that's just fine with me.

But I don't know Jack yet. I don't know who he is or what he'll be like.

I don't know if instead of crying when he hits his head on the table, he'll just yell "Bad table!" like Julia did right after she turned one.

I don't know if when we tell Jack that pulling the cats' tails isn't funny, he'll turn and mutter, "Actually, it is," with impeccable comic timing like Julia did when she was two years old.

I don't know if when I tell him to eat his sandwich over a plate so that he doesn't get crumbs on the couch, he'll shrug and say, "Sorry, dad. It's a sandwich. That's what sandwiches do," like Julia does now that she's three.

And that's why, last night, as I hovered in that place between consciousness and unconsciousness, disturbing visions of the future danced across the movie screen in my head.

I flashed forward twenty years. Jack is in college. I get a call from one of his fraternity brothers.

"Mr. Lohla, there's a problem with Jack."

"What is it?" I ask in a panic.

"Well, we were sitting around drinking beers, watching the UNC game. Everything was fine and then... well..."

"Well what?"

"Well, he just started crying," he says. "Loud, freaky crying with tears streaming down his cheeks. Most of the guys left the room, but a few of us stayed. Some just to laugh, but others to try to find out what was wrong. He wouldn't tell us. He just kept crying. It's sad, but like I said, kind of funny."

"Hang on, I'll be right there," I say, before getting in my car and speeding to his fraternity house.

When I arrive, Jack is still crying. But being his dad, I know what to do. I sit next to him, roll up my sleeve, and start whacking him on the back. This makes him cry even more, but I keep doing it.

His fraternity brothers stare at us in disbelief -- some still laughing, some horrified. There are also a few girls there, whom Jack now has no shot of ever dating. Finally, after about five minutes, Jack lets out a gigantic beer-based burp: "BAAAAAAH"!

He immediately stops crying and a smile returns to his face. A smile that is quickly replaced by a sneer.

"Come on! Go for it!" he yells at the UNC football coach, not missing a beat. "It's less than a yard! We need a touchdown!"

Unfortunately, the coach doesn't go for it. Jack smashes his beer can with his foot in disgust and tosses it into a nearby trashcan. He gives me a hug and I leave.

He should be embarrassed that he's twenty years old and has to be burped by his dad, but he's not. Because that's my son. That's my Jack.

I then flash forward even further into the future. Fifteen more years have passed. Jack is now thirty-five. I get another call. It's from his secretary Tonya.

"Mr. Lohla, there's a bit of a situation here at the office," she says.

"What's the matter?" I ask, intrigued but not worried. I'm pretty used to these calls by now.

"They were listening to a presentation in the conference room and Jack just lost it. Tears, screaming, the whole thing," she says.

"Does he have to go poo-poo?" I ask.

"Not this time. I'm pretty sure he went after his luncheon downtown," she responds.

"Did he have his nap?"

"I'm not sure. He closed the blinds and turned off the lights, but he's been a bad boy lately. He might have been on a conference call," she says.

"Weren't you watching him on his monitor?" I ask, having recently installed the same baby monitor in his office that we use now.

"I'm afraid not. He found the camera and threw it away," she says.

"Okay, I'll be right there," I say, before hopping in my car and driving to his office. When I get to his office, the receptionist gives me a sympathetic smile. She knows why I'm there.

I continue toward the boardroom to find my 35-year-old son screaming and red-faced. If Jack were just an employee, this would get him fired. However, since he's the CEO, nobody has a problem with it.

He's too worked up to nap in his office, so I know that I need to drive him around in my car. But he'll never make it down to the parking garage before reaching "total meltdown," so I have to improvise.

In the corner of the conference room, I notice one of those scooters you see advertised on TV "for those struggling with limited mobility." It belongs to his top salesman, a 53-year-old guy with a bad leg.

"May I?" I ask.

"Of course," he replies, knowing his job depends on it.

I sit on the scooter and put Jack on my back piggy-back-style, with his face resting on the back of my head and his arms wrapped around my neck. He's still crying, but as soon as I finish my first lap around the conference table, he's out like a light.

"Your son's a hell of a man," one of his employees says, trying to make me feel better about the situation. "A hell of a man. You should be proud."

I am proud. It's just that he's always been a baby and he always will be.

The employee continues. "You should be especially proud of the charitable work he's done for the 'Really Big Wussy Foundation.' As the face of that organization, he's done an extraordinary amount for really big wussies everywhere."

"And to think that we thought it was just colic," I mutter as I continue driving Jack around the conference room of his multi-million dollar company for the next thirty minutes until he wakes up rested and happy.

October 17, 2009
8:11 pm

I still don't like the guy.

ME: "Look at that thing on the horizon that just might destroy us."
JULIA: "Is it a tsunami, daddy?"
ME: "No, honey. It's Jack."

October 18, 2009
2:11 am

Possible breakthrough tonight!

After the usual five to six hours of trying to soothe and put Jack to sleep, Preva remembered something that her cousin Stacey said.

Her son Josh, who is now 21, had colic for seven months. Seven months! We're not even at *one* month! In six months, Preva and I will be insane, divorced, dead, or possibly all three.

(By the way, Josh is now the coolest, nicest guy you would want to meet, which gives us hope that Jack won't always be a screaming, squirming, insufferable blob of hate.)

Anyway, in order to get Josh to sleep, Stacey would hang a hairdryer off the side of his cradle while she rocked it with her hand or her foot if she was cooking, cleaning, or whatever.

"Get the hairdryer," Preva said.

Since she hadn't told me why yet, I assumed she was going to do her hair, go to a club, meet a guy with no kids, and live a long, happy, stress-free life with him. I couldn't blame her. I just hoped she wouldn't make me watch her try on outfits.

When she reminded me of what Stacey did, I grabbed the hairdryer. I didn't have high hopes that it would work, mainly because my ability to think positively died exactly 21 days, 18 hours, and 2 minutes ago*.

Preva laid Jack in his cradle. He was yelling, grunting, and as far from falling sleep as a baby can be. I turned the hairdryer on "high" and held it about two feet from his face. In about two seconds, his yelling and grunting stopped. Two seconds later, he opened his eyes and glared at me. Two seconds after that, he was asleep.

Preva and I looked at each other with a life and an excitement in our eyes that's pretty rare these days. She ran over to hug me, but as I started to wrap my arms around her, I accidentally pulled the plug for the hairdryer out of the wall.

Silence. Jack was still asleep. I didn't know whether to plug the hairdryer back in or not. Jack promptly answered my question for me as he woke up and his screaming picked up exactly where it left off.

I quickly plugged in the hairdryer and held it in the same spot as before. In two seconds, his yelling stopped. Two seconds later, he opened his eyes and looked at me. Two seconds after that, he was asleep.

Preva and I were elated yet dumbfounded. This time, we skipped the hug. We tried to find something to rest or dangle the hairdryer from, but the cord was too taut. So, she grabbed the yoga ball for me to sit on, which I did for another twenty minutes until I was pretty sure he would stay asleep.

This could be the start of something amazing. Maybe we found the secret. Perhaps the hairdryer is the Holy Grail, I'm Indiana Jones, and Jack is the bad guy whose face melts at the end of the movie.

I can't wait for tomorrow night to see if it is.

* Calculation done the next morning at 9:46 a.m. when ability to do math returned.

October 19, 2009
1:55 am

Shit. The hairdryer isn't the answer. It's not the Holy Grail and I'm certainly not Indiana Jones. However, I do feel older and crankier than Harrison Ford appears whenever he's on a talk show.

(Great actor, but I've never seen a celebrity who looks less interested or comfortable being interviewed. His constant shifting and pained facial expressions always make it look like he's either talking to the IRS or trying to hold in a fart.)

At any rate, it's now 1:56 am. We tried the hairdryer every thirty minutes since 10:30 pm, but it never worked. It came close to working one time, but with colic, close doesn't count. Jack finally fell asleep about ten minutes ago, due to sheer exhaustion, as he does every night.

It wasn't because of anything I did or any secret I discovered or any deal with the devil that I made in order to get him to fall asleep. It's not that I wouldn't be open to making a deal with the devil. It's just that I have no use for a shiny fiddle made of gold.

Back to the old drawing board.

My girls.
I've never had to use a hairdryer to make either of them fall asleep.

October 19, 2009
12:21 pm

I've been writing sketches for Mark and Brian for the past twelve years. I love the immediacy of radio, because I know that when I write something I'll hear it on the air the very next day. Plus, it's as fulfilling a creative outlet as I've ever had and probably ever will have.

When you write for TV, you usually don't see the result for several weeks and when you write for film, you're lucky if what you sell ever makes it to the screen. I've certainly learned that the hard way.

I collaborate with Brian on the phone several times a week, brainstorming ideas and jokes for the sketches I write. In many ways, I feel like he's my comedic soul mate and both he and Mark have been great to Preva and myself over the years.

Brian knows how busy and stressed we get, so he occasionally offers to drive out and help. It's a generous offer, and I know he truly means it, but we always decline.

Nobody should have to endure this except us, Jack's grandparents, and our awesomely competent and upbeat babysitter Stephanie, who reminds us of ourselves when we were younger and owned far fewer creatures that are dependent on us for food and solid waste removal.

Today, my conversation with Brian went like this:

ME: "I just changed Jack and now I have to finish wraps for AFV. After that, I can do that 'Red Carpet Minute' we've been talking about."
BRIAN: "I don't know how you do it."
ME: "Yeah, I don't know either. It's not easy juggling so many balls."
BRIAN: "At least they're your balls. Juggling other guys' balls would probably leave you feeling pretty dirty."
ME: "That's a great point."
Brian hears Jack crying in the background.
BRIAN: "Is that Jack crying?"
ME: "Yep."
BRIAN: "He does that a lot, huh?"
ME: "I don't know. Does 'all the time' qualify as 'a lot'?"
BRIAN: "Wow. I guess the idea with babies is that they eventually turn into actual people, right?"
ME: "That's what they tell me."
BRIAN: "Don't worry. If Jack turns out to be even half as amazing as Julia, he'll be awesome."
ME: "Thanks. But I do hate him, you understand."
BRIAN: "I completely understand."

October 21, 2009
7:47 pm

For the past fourteen years, Preva has worked for Mark and Brian, who have two million-plus listeners. She's often on the air, giving reality show updates or the female perspective when the guys discuss relationship topics.

Because it's radio, she's rarely recognized by appearance. But whenever we meet someone, especially in the Santa Clarita Valley where we live, every third or fourth person will know who she is. If the person is friendly and someone with whom we'll likely cross paths again, the conversation usually goes almost exactly like this:

THIRD OR FOURTH PERSON: "Your name's Preva? I only know one other 'Preva.' She works on the 'Mark and Brian Show'."
PREVA: "I've heard of that show. Is she fun to listen to or does she make you want to change the station?"
THIRD OR FOURTH PERSON: "No, she's great. I actually heard that she lives up here."
PREVA: "She does. I'm her."
THIRD OR FOURTH PERSON: "No. Really?"
PREVA: "Yes, really. Nice to meet you."
Etcetera....

However, if the person is rude, weird, or rubs her the wrong way, the conversation might go like this:

THIRD OR FOURTH PERSON: "Your name's Preva? I only know one other 'Preva.' She works on the 'Mark and Brian Show'."
PREVA: "Never heard of it."

It's not the kind of celebrity that gets her recognized or makes us rich, but there are cool perks like getting to meet our idols when they're interviewed on the show. (For me, Mel Brooks, Billy Crystal, and Dean Smith, the legendary coach of the UNC basketball team. For her, Rob Thomas of "Matchbox 20" and Rick Springfield. Yes, that Rick Springfield from a long, long time ago.)

It can also be a lot of fun because the people who *do* know who she is are usually extremely nice.

However, because "Preva" is such a unique name and she's spent her entire life having to spell it for people who think she's either speaking Italian or saying the name of a herpes medication, she often uses "Amy" as an alias at restaurants. I suggested she use "Georgiana, Duchess of Devonshire," but she wasn't into it.

Last night, we had an extreme case of cabin fever (mostly because that cabin was full of dirty diapers), so we decided to go eat dinner at our favorite Italian restaurant.

Since there was a wait, I stayed outside with Jack and Julia while Preva went to put our name on the list. Because she was tired, she forgot to use her trusty "Amy" alias and accidentally told the hostess "Preva."

It turns out the hostess was a Mark and Brian listener and had heard about Jack.

HOSTESS: "I hear your baby has colic."
PREVA: "Yeah, it's been pretty rough."
HOSTESS: "Mine had it, too, and nothing worked until I took him to the chiropractor."
PREVA: "That's really great. I'm just not sure that's for us."

This wasn't the first time that we had heard about a chiropractor supposedly curing colic. Some parents who've been through this swear by it. However, we just can't imagine letting a chiropractor contort Jack's spine or crack his neck, regardless of how crazy he drives us.

I wouldn't take my dog to a fortune teller, I wouldn't take my ninety-year-old grandmother to an acupuncturist, and I wouldn't take my twelve-pound baby to chiropractor.

HOSTESS: "I know it seems weird, but it really was amazing. He's like a totally different baby now."
PREVA: "When did you have your baby?"
HOSTESS: "Four months ago."
PREVA: "Four months ago? Are you serious? You look amazing."
HOSTESS: "Thank you."
PREVA: "You're welcome. We'll be outside."

Preva walked outside with a rather large scowl. I asked what took her so long. "The hostess is a listener," she said.

"Is that bad?" I asked.

"No. She took her colicky baby to a chiropractor and thinks we should, too," she grumbled.

"Do you think maybe we should? Is that why you're angry?" I inquired

"No."

"Then what is it?"

"It's because that skinny bitch had her baby four months ago!" replied my delicate flower of a wife.

"Oh," I said.

"Do you realize that I'll never be that thin again?"

"Yes, you will. It hasn't even been a month since you gave birth," I told her.

"No, I won't, Erik! I will never get that thin! It was hard after Julia was born and I'm even bigger this time! I'm nothing but boobs and loose skin! I'm disgusting!"

"Don't say that. You are *not* disgusting," I said. "Besides, she's fifteen years younger than you."

Preva shot me the kind of look that made me wish I wasn't just another dumb husband futilely searching for the right words to make his wife feel better.

"Not the right thing to say?" I asked.

"Not really," she replied.

"Didn't think so."

"You're a sharp one."

"We're not eating here, are we?" I asked, already knowing the answer.

"Nope," she said, as we promptly headed across the street to "El Pollo Loco."

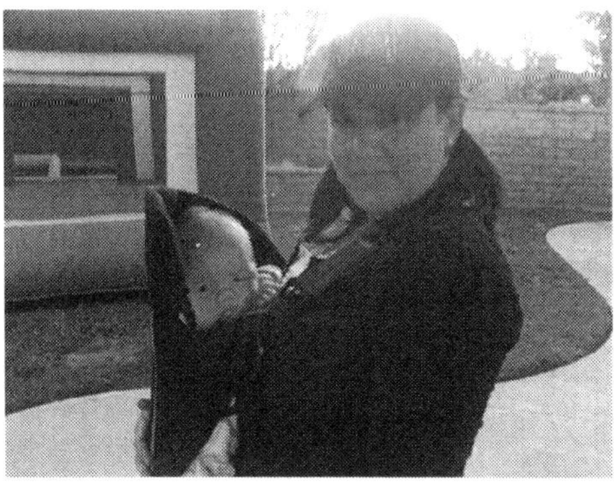

Thanks for the post-baby "fat face," Jack. No, really. That's the icing on the cake that it looks like I just ate.

October 23, 2009
12:54 am

After Julia was born, I used to joke and tell people that I paid an extra hundred dollars for a perfect baby.

Whenever friends or relatives would comment on how cute, calm, and well-behaved she was, I would say, "They don't mention it at the hospital, but if you slip the o.b. an extra hundred bucks, he'll give you a perfect baby. I was either going to spend it on that or sushi. In hindsight, I'm glad I went with the perfect baby."

But lately, in the sleep-deprived haze in which I live, I've started wondering, "Did I make up the perfect baby thing or did I actually do it?"

The birth of your first child is both an exhilarating and a head-spinning experience. With your wife in pain and your family in town, it's impossible to remember everything that happens or the order in which it occurs.

Maybe Julia is perfect because I really did give the doctor a hundred bucks. And maybe Jack isn't perfect because I didn't. If that's the case, then this is all my fault. Right now, I would give $10,000 for a baby that goes down at eight and sleeps through the night.

My advice to anyone about to give birth is to give the doctor a hundred bucks, just to be safe.

October 23, 2009
3:24 am

You know what still sucks? This.

October 24, 2009
10:18 pm

Here's something that I didn't realize until recently. Babies make you hate people.

I should be more specific. Babies don't make you hate everyone. They just make you hate your friends who don't have kids. I don't normally hate my friends. That's what makes them friends. They're people I generally respect and enjoy hanging out with. But all that has changed since Jack was born. Now I can't stand them.

Because lately, whenever I'm changing, feeding, and endlessly trying to soothe Jack, I find myself thinking about my childless friends and how they're the most selfish, self-centered, detestable people alive.

Why don't they have kids? What is it about these egotistical bastards that makes them think it's okay to go through life caring only about themselves and having fun? What kind of unfeeling and uncaring narcissistic sociopaths take a drive to Santa Barbara whenever the mood hits them? My friends who don't have kids, that's who. The pricks.

But of course, I realize all too well that they're not bad people. I wish they were, but they're not. I'm the small, petty, sleep-deprived person who can't help letting my responsibilities and lack of freedom get the best of me. I'm a little angry. I can't help it.

Tonight, I grabbed some Indian food with my good friend Jim, who's married with no kids. It was my first outing that didn't involve going to work or to Target to buy baby crap. We were having a nice time, discussing things that didn't involve babies or diapers or spitting up or babies spitting up while you were changing their diapers. And then Jim asked a simple question.

"So, what have you been up to?"

"Well, you know, pretty much just working and taking care of Jack. Having an infant is pretty crazy," I explained.

He nodded. However, I could tell that he thought that surely I *must* have more going on, but I was just too tired to go into it. Dinner continued for maybe five more minutes before he looked at me and asked, "Yeah, but what have you been *doing*?"

I won't lie. The way he said "doing" annoyed me, but I calmly explained that with work and Jack, I didn't have time to finish any screenplays or train for the marathon or backpack through Italy. Baby-care is pretty "all-consuming" and besides, I was still writing for AFV and Mark and Brian.

"Cool," he replied, but I still wasn't sure if he got it. Before I had kids, I didn't get it either.

Dinner continued and we kept stuffing our faces with Indian food. Toward the end of the meal, Jim asked about a movie script that I'd been working on.

"It's on the back-burner for now," I responded.

Jim nodded. It was the nod of a man who was either confused or frustrated by my response. It was the nod of man whose days are filled with yoga and writing and walking his dog. It was the nod of a man who, unfortunately for all of us, had one more question.

"Dude, why haven't you finished that script?"

I lost it. I shouldn't have lost it, but I lost it. And there was no way of finding it.

"Baby! Work! Work-and-a-baby!" I yelled, attacking my vegetable samosa with my fork.

Jim was taken aback. The couple at the next table was taken aback. I was embarrassed.

"Sorry," I said. "It's just that you kinda asked the same question three times."

"Sorry, man," he said. "I was just kidding."

"Gotcha," I replied. I didn't believe that he was kidding. It's not that he couldn't have been kidding, but he's not a comedy guy, and his delivery was just a little too sincere. More likely, he was just trying to make a little more conversation before the meal came to an end.

I've never had an outburst like that and I felt bad. It made me wonder. If I'm capable of such anger, should I even *have* kids?

But I'm pretty sure my anger is temporary, just like my moments of borderline insanity. Temporary anger. Temporary insanity. Temporary colic turning Jack into my temporary enemy. Everything's temporary. I just have to remember that.

October 25, 2009
2:31 am

Jack's nearly a month old. By now, I was hoping he'd be starting to go to sleep a little earlier, but unfortunately, that's not the case. He seems to love staying up late and keeping me up late.

Tonight, it occurred to me that perhaps Jack is something much darker and more mysterious than we, his doctors, or Dr. Spock had ever imagined. It occurred to me that (and maybe this is just the 2:31 a.m. talking) maybe he doesn't have colic, perhaps he's not a devil in a diaper, and he may not even have Really Big Wussy Syndrome. Maybe he's a vampire.

He sleeps during the day and he only really comes alive at night. And since he doesn't have teeth, he doesn't suck blood. He just sucks the life out of his parents.

Ever since Jack was born, I've become thin and pale with dark, sunken-in eyes. I thought it was from lack of sleep, but maybe he's slowly turning me into a vampire, too. Because that's my son. That's my Jackula.

Perhaps Bram Stoker had a colicky baby that was the inspiration for "Dracula." After all, "colic" sounds a little like "garlic."

Vampire shows are so hot right now, maybe I should write a TV show about a clan of vampire babies, whom everybody thinks have colic, that slowly take over the world.

The biggest problem is that I don't think teenage girls would find vampire babies as sexy as say, twenty-five-year-old guys with nice pecs and day-old stubble. Okay, that is a major kink in what was already a stupid idea.

I think I'll spare my manager Seth from that one. Unless he likes it and thinks he can sell it, of course. In which case, I can bang out a script by Monday.

(Speaking of vampires, we once saw Taylor Lautner who plays a werewolf in the "Twilight" vampire novels at a restaurant in town called "Wolf Creek"! Sorry you missed that one, TMZ.)

October 26, 2009
4:58 pm

Jack turned one month old today. It felt more like ten years, but it's still a milestone I'm proud of.

I'm glad we've all survived and that we're all still talking to each other. Sadly, the one person who I wish would talk won't be able to for another year or so.

It would really help my morale to hear him say, "I love you" or even "Suck it. I'm a baby. Deal with it." But babies can't talk. For a pretty Darwinian reason, all they can do is cry.

If babies just smiled or laughed when they were hungry, those babies wouldn't survive very long. Parents need to be annoyed before they tend to whatever is ailing their child and the best way to annoy them is by crying.

I don't need him to thank me for feeding, clothing, and housing him. That's why I have cats.

However, I would give a month's salary if instead of crying, Jack could smile, laugh, or even roll his eyes. Taking care of him would be so much more fun if he did the "wink and shoot a gun" thing with his thumb and forefinger whenever he peed immediately after we'd just changed his diaper.

A few minutes ago, I thought that we had the kind of breakthrough we'd been dreaming about. Preva and I were in our room, playing with Jack on our bed. By "playing," I mean that we were holding various objects over his head and guessing whether he was really looking at them or not.

All of the sudden, he slowly turned his head from the remote control I was holding over his stomach and looked at me. And then he smiled.

"Did you see that?" I excitedly asked.

"Okay, that was so cute!" Preva said. "No fair! I want him to smile at me!"

With that, Jack turned his head and smiled at her. She looked at me as her eyes instantly got watery. I don't know how girls' eyes can tear up approximately one-millionth of a second after something cute or touching happens, but they can, and it's adorable.

Preva leaned down and gave Jack a firm kiss on the lips. Jack then smiled again at me like he wanted me to do the same thing. As I started to lean forward, Jack ripped what might have been the loudest fart I've ever heard. Or at least since college, anyway.

As soon as he did, the smile disappeared from his face. It didn't disappear because he was angry or sad, just... relaxed. To our chagrin, we realized that his smile wasn't a smile. It was simply how his face dealt with the trauma of what was occurring at the other end.

We both laughed. It felt good to laugh. These days, it doesn't happen very often.

It didn't matter that Jack wasn't actually smiling. It was still gratifying to see what his face will eventually look like when he's happy and enjoying life. And it was gratifying to know that in spite of everything he's putting us through, seeing what we thought was a smile on our newborn son's face made us happier than sleeping in late or going to a movie or driving to Santa Barbara ever could.

If he makes us this crazy, then why can't we stop kissing him?

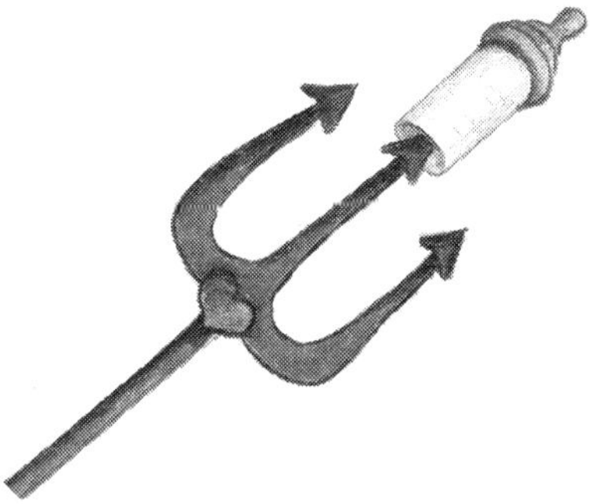

MONTH TWO

October 27, 2009
9:22 am

We named our daughter Julia after Preva's beloved grandmother, who was one of the kindest and most optimistic people she's ever known. Sadly, I never got to meet her, but I've heard many stories about how amazing she was.

It's a Jewish tradition to name children after deceased relatives, so when you combine the fact that Preva's Jewish with the fact that I've always liked the name "Julia," we had little trouble choosing her name.

With Jack, it was different. When we learned he was going to be a boy, we struggled picking a name. Just about the only name we both liked was "Jack." The only problem with it was that Preva had a grandfather named "Jack."

I say "problem" lovingly, because unlike Preva's grandmother Julia, her grandfather Jack -- or "Papa Jack" as they called him -- was the crustiest, surliest, loudest person she'd ever known. He would curse, take his pants off at parties, and when he ate shrimp, he loved throwing the tails onto other peoples' plates.

If you believe that a name can help define who a person is (and since Julia is as happy and positive as her namesake, we do), then you understand why we had serious reservations about naming him Jack. We didn't need a baby Papa Jack, but so far, that's exactly what we have.

As soon as he can, he'll be cursing, taking his diaper off at parties, and when he drinks his formula, he'll toss the bottle into other moms' diaper bags.

Maybe it's our fault. Maybe Jack is who he is because of his name.

It's doubtful that his temperament has anything to do with his middle name "Finn," which is a nod to my Finnish heritage. "Lohla" is an Americanized version of my grandfather's Finnish name, which had about twenty-eight more vowels before my grandfather shortened it.

Unlike *our* Finn, Finnish people tend to be rather stoic, reserved individuals not prone to outbursts of emotion. Unfortunately, Finland has one of the highest suicide rates of any country, so maybe it would do them some good not to keep everything so bottled up.

Occasionally, parents will name their kids after the city in which they were conceived. We'd considered doing that for Jack's middle name, but since he was conceived at home, that wasn't an option.

I'm not supposed to say *where* in our house, but let's just say that if we named him after the type of closet where he was conceived, his middle name would be "Walken."

October 27, 2009
8:07 pm

Julia has a little pink stuffed elephant named "Ellie." She loves Ellie more than she loves us. It's like a drug to her. When Julia holds Ellie to her face and inhales, a serenity passes over her that's so instant and so powerful, it must be filled with cupcakes.

Julia, Ellie, and Snort.

Preva and I have both awakened in cold sweats after having nightmares about losing Ellie and how traumatized Julia would be. Today, those nightmares came true.

This morning, we drove to a small, rural town called "Acton" to get swine flu shots. Hopefully, swine flu will end up being one of those illnesses whose danger has been overhyped by the media. We don't usually fall victim to this kind of fear mongering, but with a newborn in the house, we're susceptible to pretty much any kind of mongering.

We parked and got in line along with hundreds of other people. The best part of our line was that it ran right alongside a horse pasture, which meant that every five minutes Julia would pick up a petrified horse turd, thinking it was a rock.

Somehow, telling a three-year-old that a rock is actually a horse turd encourages, rather than dissuades, them to pick it up. She was beyond fascinated.

"Why is horse poop so hard?!" and "Doesn't it hurt coming out?!" she yelled as she stared at it, her eyes squinted and nose crinkled in fascination.

We explained that horse poop gets hard from being out in the sun for so long and that we would likely be just as hard and crusty by the time we got our shots.

We finally reached the nurses' tent where we gave them our information before going inside to get our "swine flu spray," which would be shot into our nostrils. Somehow, a swine flu spray seemed less effective than a swine flu shot. I guess I should just be glad we weren't given the swine flu lip balm.

It was then that I heard Julia utter the dreaded words, "Where's Ellie?"

Minutes earlier, I had mistakenly let Julia carry Ellie instead of leaving her in the stroller as I was told. Preva glared at me, "I don't believe this!" (Translation: "You're the reason Ellie's gone and I will never forgive you.")

We frantically searched a fifty-yard radius of where we were the last time I remember seeing Ellie in Julia's clutches, but to no avail. I jumped up on a stone wall and announced to a large portion of the line: "Has anyone seen a little pink stuffed elephant?!"

I got several odd looks, before I realized that I needed to add, "It's my daughter's!"

They called our names. It was time for our sprays. We wanted to continue our search, but knew we had to go or lose our turn in line. Preva was on the verge of tears when the nurse said, "There's nothing to be scared of."

We knew she was wrong. Losing Ellie would be the end of the world to our three-year-old and that was the scariest thing that either of us could imagine.

After asking every nurse, volunteer, and non-Spanish speaking person in line if they'd seen a little pink elephant, we reluctantly got into the car. As we drove away, the reality that we'd lost Ellie still hadn't hit Julia, but Preva and I both had huge pits in our stomachs.

"Where's Ellie?" Julia asked again as we headed toward the highway.

"I can't believe how I feel right now," Preva said. "I thought we'd have Ellie forever," she added, choking up.

I felt the same way, because I knew what that elephant meant to Julia. It was like a piece of her childhood was suddenly gone and it truly hurt. I reached over and held Preva's hand as we pulled into a McDonald's drive-thru.

"It's going to be alright," I told her as she wiped away a tear. I then turned and looked at my sweet little girl, who had no idea that her beloved Ellie was probably gone forever.

"What's the matter, daddy?" she asked.

I don't know whether it was her lack of understanding of the gravity of the situation or just the way she said "daddy," but I lost it. I started bawling.

Somehow, losing that elephant had unleashed all of the pent-up frustrations and emotions that had been building up in both of us. In a way, it was cathartic. But it wasn't worth what was in store for us later when we would have to explain to our heartbroken daughter that her best friend wasn't coming home. I pulled up to the speaker.

"Welcome to McDonald's. Would you like to try our chicken snack wrap?" a cheery female voice asked.

"No, thank you," I said, in between sobs.

"Excuse me?" she asked.

"I don't want to try the chicken snack wrap!" I said much louder, hoping the increased volume would disguise my crying. But it only made it more obvious.

"It's okay, sir. Please calm down. You don't have to try the chicken snack wrap," she responded, believing it was her menu suggestion that set me off.

"I'm sorry. My daughter lost her favorite elephant today and we're all a little emotional," I explained.

There was a brief pause before she finally said, "I understand. What *would* you like to order?"

I took a deep breath and managed to compose myself long enough to give her our order. She gave me my total and I pulled forward.

"Window please," Julia chirped, wanting me to roll down her backseat window so that she could talk to the person working the drive-thru, as she likes to do.

We pulled up to the window. The teenage girl who'd taken our order said, "I'm so sorry" as Preva and I tried to hide our red eyes with Kleenex. She then looked in the backseat, expecting to see an equally distraught little girl.

"Hi! What your name?" Julia asked as cheerily as humanly possible.

The girl looked at us, clearly confused, before saying, "Karen." She then asked Julia, "How are you today?"

"Did you know horse poop is really hard?" Julia asked.

"No, I didn't," replied Karen.

"My poop's not hard, but horse poop is really hard. And big, too," she said, smiling as big as she possibly could.

Karen wasn't sure how to respond to that, which is probably why she didn't. There was a sudden change in her demeanor. Gone was the look of sympathy as she looked at me and said, "That'll be $12.43."

As I handed her a twenty, I could tell she thought I made up the whole thing about losing Ellie. She probably thought I was trying to cover up a much darker and stranger reason why two adults were crying while their three-year-old daughter was obsessed with horse poop.

Karen handed me my change and a few moments later our food, and we pulled away.

My weeping stopped. My sadness had subsided, but in its place was anger. Maybe it was good that we lost Ellie, I thought. It was a good lesson for Julia to learn that life is full of loss and despair. I took Julia's cheeseburger out of her Happy Meal, unwrapped it, and stared at it.

"What are you doing?" Preva asked nervously.

"Nothing," I said.

"You sure about that?"

I nodded, but I wasn't sure. I hadn't eaten red meat in eight years. I hadn't even had a fleeting desire to, yet I was suddenly consumed with an overwhelming desire to take a big bite out of Julia's cheeseburger. I wasn't sure why.

Maybe I just felt like acting out, or that eating red meat would help me return to my primal roots where I would be free from painful feelings like anger, guilt, and regret that arise from losing a stupid little stuffed pink elephant.

"I don't like the way you're looking at that cheeseburger, Lohla," my wife deadpanned.

"Everything dies. Nothing matters," I said, staring off into the distance. "They call it a 'Happy Meal.' Talk about irony."

"Okay, that's about enough," Preva said, putting an end to my melodramatic self-pity.

I took one last look at the cheeseburger before handing it to Julia, who happily started munching it.

An hour after we got home, we got a call from the swine flu center. Someone had found Ellie and turned her in. Fortunately, grandma had sewed our phone number onto Ellie's stomach in the event of just such a catastrophe.

We were overjoyed. Preva ran into my arms as if I were a recently released hostage. We hadn't hugged like that since we found out that Jack was going to be a boy

We'd narrowly averted tragedy. We'd almost had to teach Julia the most painful lesson of her life. I'd nearly eaten a cheeseburger.

Still, we accomplished two important things. The first was getting vaccines so that we weren't susceptible to the "swine flu virus." The second was deciding that Ellie always stays in the car so that we can't get "lost elephant disease."

Simpler, more "stuffed animal-free" times.
But there were still plenty of real ones around.

October 28, 2009
9:33 pm

Last night around midnight (while I was trying to stay awake and sane while holding Jack), I decided that there should be a cable channel for parents of difficult newborns. A channel that would entertain, comfort, and make parents realize that they're not bad people for wanting this phase of babyhood to be OVER.

Here are some examples of the type of programming the "Newborn Network" would have:

"CSI (Cranky Son Investigation): Valencia"
"America's Most Depressing Home Videos"
"Extreme Infant Makeover"
"The (I Wish I Was Still A) Bachelor"
"How I Met Your Mother's Psychiatrist"
"Buffy the Colicky Baby Slayer"
"The Real Colicky Babies of Orange County"
"So You Think You Can Soothe A Baby"
"Crazy House on the Prairie"
"Are You Smarter than a Three-Week Old?"
"MTV (Baby Hates His) Cribs"
"Colic, Texas Ranger"

The "Food Network" makes you hungry, the "E Channel" makes you want to throw something at a Kardashian, and the "Newborn Network" would make parents of colicky babies realize that they're not alone.

It would also be the perfect channel for teenagers to make them never ever want to have sex.

October 29, 2009
12:44 pm

It just hit me. I know what this is like. The complete physical, mental, and emotional exhaustion that you feel almost every second of almost every day. Having a cranky newborn is like driving home from Las Vegas.

The fun, exhilarating, "mama-need-a-new-pair-of-shoes" yin of Las Vegas is directly opposed by the grueling, painful, "daddy-needs-a-new-liver" yang of the drive home.

When you drive home from Las Vegas, you're incredibly tired and absolutely everything hurts. Your feet hurt, your brain hurts, and your wallet really hurts. Each day I spend with Jack is like driving home from Vegas. Except that instead of the drive lasting five hours, it lasts twenty-four hours.

I think that's the real reason California's bankrupt. It's just too close to Las Vegas.

If you've ever driven home from Vegas, then you know exactly how I feel. You constantly ask yourself questions like "Why did I drink that?" "Why did I eat that?" "Why did I bet that?' "Why did I let my friend talk me into drinking even more of that?" and, of course, "Why do I even go when I know that I'll just end up feeling like this?"

You can't help but wonder whether the amount of fun you had there was worth the amount of pain you're experiencing now. Was the forty-eight hours of fun worth this hellish four to ten-hour drive home? I'm not proud, but it's same thing with Jack. I wonder whether the thirty minutes of fun (okay, three minutes) we had conceiving him was worth this.

I'm simultaneously the world's most boring talk show host and talk show guest as I constantly ask myself questions like, "Should we have done this?" "Are we too old to be doing this?" and "What was it like working with Cate Blanchett?"

I'm too tired to be asking these questions and I'm definitely too tired to be answering them with a response that doesn't depress me even further. Even a drive home from Vegas with a hangover, three smelly friends, and no money in my wallet is easier than this.

When things get better -- if things better -- I'll be able to say that this was a good idea. But until then, it's very hard to say that it was.

Enough with the crying baby, already. We're tired, we're jammied, we're ready for bed.

October 30, 2009
10:30 am

I'm not on Facebook, but here's a quick "JackBook" status update:

"Babies give you something to live for... like vacations without them when they're old enough to stay with grandma."

October 30, 2009
4:50 pm

I don't know why, but I just tried again. I put a pacifier in Jack's mouth to try and soothe him, but he spit it right out. I'm officially done trying.

I feel like a lot of this crying could be averted if he would just suck on that stupid thing. That's all it would take. But Jack won't even do that, precisely because he knows we want him to.

I don't know what it is, but neither of my kids would let us put a pacifier in their mouths for even a second.

Julia never cried, but on the few occasions where she was constipated and looked uncomfortable, we tried putting a pacifier in her mouth while we pumped her legs and tried to squeeze one out, Play-Doh Fun Factory-style. (Julia, if you're reading this as a teenager, you're welcome.) But it simply didn't take.

Jack cries constantly, so we've alternately tried placing, sticking, and shoving pacifiers in his mouth. We've tried all sorts of different pacifiers with all sorts of different shapes and textures. It doesn't matter. He hates all of them and he hates us for trying.

We always roll our eyes when we see five-year-olds walking around the mall with pacifiers in their mouths. But now, we get it.

I wouldn't mind seeing Jack go to his high school prom with the prom queen on his arm and a pacifier in his mouth if it meant that we all could get more sleep.

We even tried sticking his thumb in his mouth to prematurely create a bad habit, but that didn't work either. Perhaps his thumb was just too small or maybe he simply thought that us dipping his thumb in Preva's breast milk to make it tastier was just plain weird. I know Preva did.

October 31, 2009
12:05 pm

No matter where I am, Jack is always in the next room. He's not, of course, but his screaming has burned itself into my brain so that I hear him wherever I go.

For the first month of his life, whenever I heard him wail I would literally stand up to go check on him, whether I was at work, Starbucks, or Jiffy Lube.

That's the closest I've come to thinking that I was literally going crazy, because I couldn't have been more positive that I was actually hearing Jack cry.

Now, I'm a little better at knowing whether or not I'm hearing actual crying and telling whether it's Jack's, Preva's, or mine.

October 31, 2009
11:03 pm

Tonight was Halloween. Julia went as a princess. Jack went as a chicken. I went as a dad who hasn't had a decent night's sleep in 35 days.

Actually, I went as a dead Braves fan with a baseball bat handle sticking through his forehead. Not sure why.

November 2, 2009
10:39 pm

Today, Julia learned what the word "dead" means.

A few months ago, we TiVo'd a Michael Jackson music video marathon that VH1 ran soon after he died. Julia loves dancing, so naturally, she loves watching Michael's signature moves.

This morning, we were all in the living room. Julia was watching Michael Jackson videos, Preva was feeding Jack, and I was inhaling breakfast and injecting coffee as I prepared to leave for work.

After watching her favorite video, "Black and White," Julia announced that she'd like to meet Michael Jackson. Preva and I looked at each other, unsure of what to say.

Because I was too tired to know better, I turned to Julia and said, "I'm sorry, but you can't meet Michael Jackson. He's dead."

Preva gasped. Julia gave me a puzzled look. "What's 'dead'?" she asked.

"It means that he's not alive. He doesn't eat or watch TV or go to school anymore."

"Like the dinosaurs?" Julia asked.

"That's right," Preva answered. "Michael Jackson's up in the clouds with the dinosaurs."

Julia looked proud that she understood, but also sad because of what it meant. I felt the same way. I was proud of my little girl, but also sad that her innocence was slowly being chipped away.

"But I want to meet Michael Jackson," Julia said, an adorable little tear forming in her adorable little eye.

Well, that was a bit too much for Preva. She started bawling.

"Right now?!" she asked, half-crying and half-laughing. "You're leaving for work and I have to spend all day explaining that Michael Jackson's dead?! Thanks a lot!"

I laughed and then looked at Jack, squirming and grunting in Preva's arms. He's almost a year away from being able to talk, but before I know it, he'll be asking what "dead" means.

Later in the day, I got a call at work. We were in the middle of pitching jokes for a video of a ferret trying to get out of a laundry basket. "Ferrets aren't funny" is one of my boss Todd Thicke's mottos. But to tell you the truth, I think he stole that from Mark Twain.

In case you're wondering, Todd is Alan Thicke's equally handsome and accomplished brother. He also has the exact same voice as Alan, which is pretty funny for my fellow writers and I who grew up watching "Growing

Pains." It's even funnier when he tells us that we need to come up with a good nut hit pun or we can forget about going to the prom.

I looked at my phone. It was Preva. She rarely calls me at work, so I figured it might be an emergency. I picked up the phone. "Hello?"

"Hi, honey. Do you have a minute?" she asked.

"Yeah, is everything okay?"

"I'm sorry for calling you at work, but I just had to tell you something really quick," she said.

"Okay. But first, do you have any good ferret puns?" I asked.

"Huh?"

"Never mind. Go ahead," I said.

Preva proceeded to tell me that she and the kids had just gone clothes shopping at Old Navy. While they were walking back to the car, Julia was about to step out into the street before Preva stopped her.

"Julia! Don't ever walk in the street without holding my hand! You could get hit by a car!" Preva said, grabbing Julia's hand.

"Thanks, mommy," Julia answered, appreciatively. "If a car hit me, I'd be flattened like a pancake. Then I'd be up in clouds with the dinosaurs and Michael Jackson."

Preva started laughing along with two other moms who were waiting to cross the street.

"Did she just say what I think she said?" one mom asked.

"Yup," Preva replied.

"She knows who Michael Jackson is?" the other mom asked.

"Yeah, she loves him. But she thinks his dad Joe is an a-hole," Preva whispered.

"Really?" the mom asked, laughing.

"No, but when she's a little older, I'll make sure she knows that he is."

I got a good laugh from the story and thanked her for calling to tell me about it. I then relayed the tale to the other three writers in the writers' room.

"That's pretty funny," my friend Mike replied. "But you know what would really be great? A joke about a ferret getting out of a laundry basket."

"Right," I said, re-focusing on the task at hand.

November 3, 2009
10:55 am

I just got finished talking with Brian about tomorrow's sketch. Here's the nitty-gritty on how that went down.

BRIAN: "I gotta run, but text me if you need any more punchies."
ME: "Cool. What are you doing today?"
BRIAN: "Oh, let's see…"
ME: "Wait. Do I want to know?"
BRIAN: "Maybe not."
ME: "What the hell? Indulge me."
BRIAN: "Going to play eighteen holes with Gary and then I'm taking a date to Mastro's."
ME: "So, you're playing golf and then taking a beautiful girl to one of the best restaurants in L.A., which will likely be followed by sex? Yeah, maybe I didn't want to know that."
BRIAN: "Yeah. Hmm.... Okay! Good talk!"
ME: "Yep. Great talk. Goodbye."

November 3, 2009
9:31 pm

Four years ago, Preva and I flew to Atlanta to visit my best friend Pete, whose son Luke was turning one. I showed her where I grew up and went to school, and except for the birds who chirped literally all night long, we had a great time.

I watched in amazement as Pete changed Luke's big poopy diaper while carrying on a conversation with me about the Braves as if he were trying his shoes or eating a sandwich or doing something that wasn't nearly as disgusting as changing a big poopy diaper.

"How do you that?" I asked, averting my eyes from the poop and breathing through my mouth.

"After a while, you don't even think about it," he said.

I rolled my eyes as I watched my childhood friend hold the new diaper in his mouth while simultaneously sprinkling baby powder on his son's balls and tossing the dirty diaper in the diaper pail.

I admired Pete for being a good dad, but mainly, I felt sorry for him. In my head, I was thinking, "I'll change my baby's diapers, but not the poopy ones. Mom gets the poopy ones. If that's the only thing I put my foot down on, I'm pretty sure I can get away with it." Turns out, I couldn't.

I'm not big on poop. Never have been. I realize it's gotten plenty of attention in this book, but that's just because I'm reporting the truth.

On "America's Funniest Home Videos," we see videos that contain practically every substance that a person's body can produce. I'm okay with, even entertained by, all of those. But when I screen a video of a toddler finger-painting his room with his own you-know-what I get a little queasy.

Anyway, the thought that I could get away with being a great, hands-on parent without having to deal with poopy diapers amuses me to this day. That's how out of touch I was with the reality of being a parent. Being a parent is like skydiving. It's impossible to know what it's like until you try it. By the way, I've never skydived. But if I did, I'm pretty sure somebody would need to change *my* poopy diaper.

Did I really think that every time Julia made a brown present, I could create a scenario where Preva would notice it before me, and thereby feel more obligated to handle it? I wasn't sure how to do that. What I *was* sure of is that simply saying, "I'm not big on poop" wouldn't free me of the "duty." Pun intended.

However, Pete was right. I've now taken care of so many of Julia's and child number two's "number two's" that it hardly bothers me at all. I don't gag or avert my eyes or let them ripen on the butt vine in hopes the responsibility will fall to Preva. Sometimes I don't even wash my hands after I change him, which is no small feat in light of my mild obsessive compulsiveness.

It's amazing how kids can change you from being the person you are to the person you have to be, which is almost always an improvement.

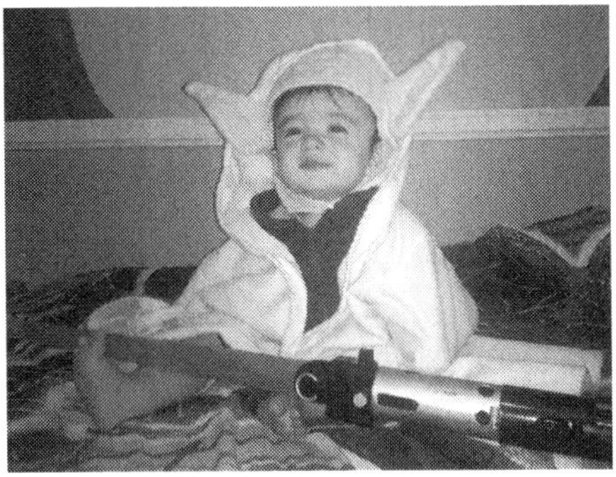

Yoda-Jack: "Crazy will I make you.
There is no pee. Only doo."

November 5, 2009
12:22 am

I don't know who invented the "Baby Bjorn," but I want to smack him in the face with a soggy diaper. I would never hit a girl, so if a woman invented it, I would ask Preva to do it for me.

For those who don't know, a Baby Bjorn is a soft, sling-like, baby-carrying device, which lets you carry your child against your chest. It relieves stress on your back and shoulders and leaves your arms free so that you can eat, shop, or go to the bathroom while holding your baby.

In the interest of full disclosure, I have eaten and shopped, as well as eaten and used the bathroom while wearing a Baby Bjorn. The only thing I *haven't* done with it is shop while using the bathroom, but I'm so tired these days, I wouldn't be surprised if it happened.

Anyway, it's a great invention and when Jack's having a fit, sticking him in the Bjorn is the only thing that works.

The problem is that there are a seemingly infinite number of straps, buttons, and buckles, which makes putting it on a major pain in the ass.

By the time I've figured out how to put it on, any stress I've relieved in my shoulders has been negated by the anxiety that's formed in my brain. I don't know where to put my head, which hole my arm goes through, or whether I'm supposed to fasten the bottom buckles before or after Jack is inside.

If I do the buckle before he's inside, the Bjorn is too snug to squeeze Jack into and if I do it after Jack's inside, he blocks my view of the buckle apparatus and I can't get the one part to snap inside the other part.

My frustration is compounded by the fact that whenever I use the Bjorn, I'm so tired that I can barely stand up.

The legendary tennis player Bjorn Borg is from Sweden. I'm not sure if the Baby Bjorn comes from Sweden, but if it is, here's what I picture...

Unlike Americans, who pass the time on their iPhones, I think Swedes sit on the subway or spend their lunch breaks trying to figure out how to properly put on a Baby Bjorn. Some of the people don't even have babies. They just use baby-sized Swedish meatballs.

I'm pretty sure the Baby Bjorn doesn't have a patent. Because even with instructions and a blueprint, I doubt anyone at the U.S. patent office could figure out how it worked and consequently wouldn't know what made it unique and worth patenting.

If I worked there, I certainly wouldn't give it a patent. But I continue to use it. Because when my back is killing me and I'm too tired to drive Jack around or take him in the shower, it's the only thing that works.

I hate the Baby *Bjorn*. But in the end, I'm glad we *bjought* one. (By the way, the silent "j" in "Bjorn" stands for "Jack" who's anything BUT silent.)

Eating a turkey*bjurger*.

November 5, 2009
10:56 pm

I wait 37 years for a son and when he finally gets here, he's a dick.

November 6, 2009
1:44 am

Tonight, I was too tired to hold Jack, carry him in the Bjorn, or even drive him around. So we hung out in the garage. He cried his eyes out while I swept up mouse turds using an old issue of "Sports Illustrated" as a dustpan. Every time I stood up, the blood rushed to my delirious head, nearly causing me to pass out.

On nights like these, I wish I had other options.

If I were an eccentric British billionaire like Richard Branson, I would start something called "The Infant Express." It would be a large, luxury, decked-out bus that would run from eight at night until six in the morning for cranky infants and their parents.

The babies would be free to cry as much as they wanted and their parents would be free to do all of the things they don't have the time or opportunity to do at home when they're trying to keep their babies calm, quiet, and happy. Did I say "calm, quiet, and happy"? I meant "fed, safe, and alive."

I'm not talking about anything crazy. Nothing scandalous. Nothing that would keep Charlie Sheen entertained. Just a place where parents could watch a movie or check their email without worrying about their screaming baby waking their spouse, their other children, or their spiteful cats who like peeing on things.

Actually, if I were a British billionaire, I'd make sure the bus also had a dentist onboard, since every Brit on TV looks like they could use their teeth as a can opener.

November 6, 2009
12:11 pm

For the past few hours, I've been writing leads for AFV. "Leads" are the things that our extremely talented and ridiculously down-to-earth host Tom Bergeron utters to introduce the videos.

Preva just poked her head into my office to make sure I'm working and not asleep, because she knows that today I don't have time for a nap, even a short one.

PREVA: "Finish your leads?"
ME: "Yep."
PREVA: "How's the diary coming?"
ME: "Good. And it's a book."
PREVA: "Sure wish I had time to write a diary."
ME: "Book."
PREVA: "I know the point is to describe how tired and busy you are. But if you're that tired and busy, how do you have time to write a diary?"
ME: "Good time management."
PREVA: "Huh?"
ME: "I recently decided to cut out eating and blinking. It's amazing how much time that saves."
PREVA: "Uh-huh. When you get a chance, can you empty the diaper pail? It stinks."

November 7, 2009
2:39 pm

Jack, Jack, Jack...

In spite of it all, I love you more than the sun. I love you more than the moon. I love you *almost* as much elderly Asian couples who I see taking their nightly stroll, where both the husband and wife are wearing pajamas and the wife is walking a good fifteen feet in front of her husband.

And I *really* love that, so that's saying a lot.

November 7, 2009
8:12 pm

Jack's getting bigger.

When you're with your kids all the time, it's impossible to notice all the subtle changes. But at certain moments, it really hits me just how much larger he is than when we brought him home.

Suddenly, when I hand him to Preva at the end of our shower (which still only soothes him while he's actually *in* it, by the way), she has to bend her knees to take his weight. Suddenly, when I put him in his crib, he doesn't look like a Ken doll in an Olympic-sized pool.

His thighs aren't as chubby, his toes aren't as stubby, and his eyes aren't as squinty. Overall, he's not the tiny, flabby, red-faced ball of hate that he was. And I kind of miss it.

That's how I know that in spite of everything, I love him. Because as impossible as he was and as rocky as the road continues to be, it still makes me sad to think that I'll never have a child that small again.

He's our last baby. Preva had her tubes tied when Jack was taken out, so it's certain that we've launched the last of the Lohla's. And I'm fine with that.

But it does make me emotional to think that with every inch and every milestone, that will be the last time we have a baby that size and the last time we see that milestone being reached.

I can't wait until we all start sleeping more, so that we can fully appreciate and enjoy all the little changes. But somehow, even in the midst of this madness, I can almost understand how people would want to have another baby even after having a baby like ours.

I have no idea how he's able to make me feel that way, but he does. Because that's my son. That's my Jack

Of course my grandma loves him. She's in Michigan and she's 90. When he cries, she doesn't hear a damn thing.

November 8, 2009
9:51 pm

No matter how trying our day is, we can always count on Julia to make us laugh.

Tonight, as I was getting out of the shower with Jack, Julia pointed at my groin and started laughing. "Your privates look funny," she said.

Perfect. It was a rough day, filled with even more frustration than usual. All I needed now was someone making fun of my penis. Nevertheless, I had to bite.

"Funny how?" I asked, intrigued.

"It looks like they're going poo," she said matter-of-factly.

I looked down at my privates and laughed, somehow never having drawn a parallel between the shape of my package with a "number two." I laughed and assured her that it was not, in fact, "poo," while reminding her that boys' privates and girls' privates simply look different.

I then directed her attention to Jack's area and said, "See? It looks like Jack's privates are going poo, too."

"Yeah," she nodded. "But it looks like he didn't eat as much."

I laughed as I decided that three was the age she would start only showering with mom.

November 10, 2009
2:35 am

This is the only entry in this book that will be intentionally humor-free. All of the others are written to at least make you smile. Or, if you're the parent of a newborn, to at least *think* about smiling if you don't even have the energy to actually do it.

But what I'm wondering at the moment is, why isn't there a hotline for frustrated parents of infants, especially for those of infants like Jack?! I'm sure there are people or organizations you can talk to, but I'm talking about a nationally advertised hotline that everybody knows about.

Preva always says that there needs to be a number that moms and dads can call when they're holding a screaming baby and feeling exhausted, helpless, and alone. They would be connected to someone who's been there. Someone with advice or a kind word who could talk them off the ledge before they end up doing something harmful to themselves or their child, whether intentional or unintentional. She's couldn't be more right.

We have a great marriage and our parents were amazing role models, yet it's almost too much for us at times. I can't even imagine how people with no partner or support system handle this. Half the time when I stare bleary-eyed at Jack, that's who I'm thinking about. There needs to be someone they can call.

When you have a baby, they should give you a phone number for stressed-out parents at their wits' end. The nurses should make you memorize it before you're even allowed to leave the hospital. If you can't memorize it, they should tattoo it on your arm. It should be a part of Obama's new healthcare plan. There should be a national ad campaign so that everyone knows the number.

I'm sure there will never be something like that. It would probably be too expensive. But if you've ever been driven half-crazy by a baby or you know someone who has, then you know that it would be worth whatever it cost.

I don't know. Maybe Oprah would pay for it.

November 10, 2009
11:44 pm

Some people believe that the best reason to have kids is so that you have someone to take care of you when you get older. "Someone willing to wipe my butt when I'm old," as they say. But here's the problem. By the time you finally *need* them to take care of you, you're too old to actually *enjoy* it.

That's why I'm going to start pooping in a diaper when I'm 53. Why 53? Forcing Jack to change me when he's just getting his driver's license will be the perfect payback for what he's doing to me now.

"Want to borrow the car? Sure thing. But before you do, guess what? Daddy made a stinky."

Too tired to say cheese, spell cheese, or even think about cheese.

November 11, 2009
12:45 am

Mark from the show knows exactly what we're going through. He had a colicky baby, too.

His second child Amy had colic and even though she's now in college, he and his wife Lynda still remember every frustrating and exhausting second like it was yesterday.

But here's why Mark has a heavier and more impressive set of balls hanging off him than I do. He had a colicky baby and he STILL went on to have another child after that!

And Lynda has a more impressive… well, a more impressive whatever the female equivalent of balls are than Preva.

November 11, 2009
2:01 am

I'm writing this as I lie on the floor flat on my back.

I finally got Jack to fall asleep and put him in his cradle. Now my back is so sore, I can no longer sit up, let alone stand up.

My arms are nearly too weak to type and my knees are shaking so much from three hours of walking and bouncing up and down, they can barely support the laptop I have leaning against them.

I know babies are murder on a mother's body, but they're at the very least manslaughter on mine.

I've never had back problems. But every so often, I now feel a crippling twinge in my lower back that nearly drops me to the floor. My knees have never hurt a day in my life. But lately, my right knee occasionally locks up in such a way that it doesn't properly bend again until the next day.

"Cry me a river," is Preva's typical response when I mention my trick knee to her. "At least *every* part of your body isn't completely jacked."

She's right. Still, I find it hard to believe I haven't done permanent damage to at least one of these body parts that now twinges, pops, or aches for the first time in my life. I feel at least ten years older than I did just two months ago.

November 12, 2009
9:44 am

I'm still hurting. It's not the first morning that I've woken up and still been sore from the night before.

Since I don't have time to go to the gym anymore, I'd like to think that every night is a workout and that carrying and appeasing Jack is actually getting me in better shape. But I'm not getting stronger. I'm just wearing down.

At 37 years old, I know that I'm not that old. But I'm also not that young. I'm not a "Type A" personality and I've never been accused of being what you'd call a "high energy" person, but I'm pretty sure I'd have a little more "oomph" to deal with everything Jack throws at me if I were ten or fifteen years younger. To quote too many cops in too many cop movies, "I'm gettin' too old for this shit."

I could smoke and eat red meat as I'm talking on a cell phone from the early 1990's while not wearing sunscreen on the hottest day of the year and then go party with Lindsay Lohan all night and *still* age less quickly than Jack's aging me right now.

Overall, I just feel... old.

It's not the kind of "old" that makes me watch "Matlock" or play shuffleboard, but occasionally -- from out of nowhere and without warning -- I'll look out my front window in hopes of seeing kids playing, so that I could yell at them to get the hell off my lawn.

November 13, 2009
3:13 am

Would life be easier and more enjoyable right now if we didn't have a three-year-old and a one-month old? Yes. Will life be better and more fun because of our kids...

A) Five...
B) Ten...
C) Twenty...
D) Thirty...
E) Or even forty years from now?

Answers:

A) I sure hope so.
B) I sure think so.
C) Probably.
D) I'm 99% sure.
E) Of course.

Unlike any of our financial investments over the past five years, this one will actually pay off.

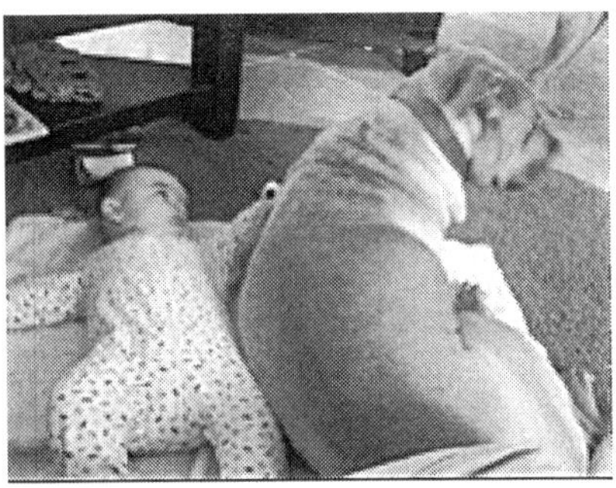

"Here's the deal. If you make Bentley do a trick, make sure it's not, 'Roll over'."

November 13, 2009
10:50 pm

Preva was a cheerleader in high school. She loved watching the guys, jumping up and down, and kicking her legs high in the air to impress them. Sometimes she would even do those things while she was cheerleading.

In high school, I was too shy to even date. Little did I know that fourteen years later and three thousand miles away, I would end up marrying a spunky and beautiful former head cheerleader.

Preva enjoys sports. But unfortunately for her, she married one of those guys who thinks that sports are the most important thing in the world... if for no other reason than they are.

She often questions whether or not I really love her and the kids, because I never get more excited or more depressed than when my team wins or loses.

I jump up and down on the couch, I throw soft objects at walls (If I were capable of patching or painting walls, I would throw hard ones), and every year when the Atlanta Braves are knocked out of the playoffs, I get in the car and drive around for three hours while I attempt to pick up the pieces of my shattered life and put them back together.

Since Preva sleeps in the same room as Jack, she's gotten into the habit of falling asleep to ESPN on TV. For her, the nonstop sports highlights are boring enough to put her to sleep, yet loud enough to drown out Jack's nonstop grunting, whining, and whimpering.

But recently, a funny thing started happening. In the mornings, instead of greeting me with the usual "Here's your son, I need to pump" or "Julia's crying because she has diarrhea," she would say things like "I think the

Yankees offense is too much for the Phillies" or "Childress needs to sit Brett Favre more if he wants to save his shoulder for the playoffs."

Her passing interest in sports had suddenly morphed into something that, if properly nurtured, could become the kind of unhealthy, time-wasting obsession that I currently enjoy. Before she conked out, she was processing sports facts, which further entered her subconscious after she was asleep.

To a husband for whom the World Series is like Christmas and March Madness is like Halloween, Thanksgiving, and Secretary Appreciation Day all rolled into one, this was a dream come true. If anything could make Jack's colic worth it, it was this.

With dirty diapers, crusty baby bottles, and smelly jammies all over the place, our home had quickly turned into the worst sports bar in the universe. But at least it was a sports bar.

I already knew that I'd married my best friend, but now she was a best friend who cared about whether a few smart moves in free agency could get the Braves back to the World Series. It was different. It was better. I should have known it was too good to last.

Last Friday, while I was holding Jack, desperately trying to soothe him so as not to wake Julia, I heard from the other room a frantic, "Erik!"

I ran into our bedroom, thinking that something was terribly wrong. I entered to find Preva lying in bed, safe but miserable.

"I can't get to sleep!" she said, frantic.

"What's the matter?" I asked, as she pointed at the television, which was broadcasting ESPN as usual. I still didn't understand what was wrong, unless she was simply frightened by NFL draft guru Mel Kiper Jr.'s thick, lion-like mane of jet-black hair.

She sighed. "It doesn't work anymore."

I instantly knew what she meant. She had simply become too interested in sports for it to work as background noise. I panicked.

"Please, honey?! Please try again!" I implored, fearing I would soon lose the new and improved, sports-obsessed wife that she had become.

"It won't work," she said, shaking her head.

"Don't say that!" I begged. "They'll be talking about hockey soon! Even I could fall asleep to that!"

With Jack and I looking on, she calmly picked up the remote control and aimed it at the television. Before I could even start crying, ESPN was gone. Just like that.

In its place was a Korean soap opera with Korean actors speaking Korean. As far as I could tell, none of the actors were discussing whether the Cavaliers could win an NBA championship before LeBron bolts Cleveland. And the next morning, neither were we.

Our daily sports conversations have slowly returned to the usual conversations about reality shows and our observations about how we wouldn't eat anything cooked by that Gordon Ramsay a-hole from "Hell's Kitchen," because he yells so much that he probably spits in everything he cooks.

But it's okay. I'll always cherish the week or so that my wife cared just as much about sports as me.

That doesn't mean I don't occasionally turn to ESPN after she falls asleep in hopes it will seep into her brain while she's unconscious.

Honey, if you ever end up reading this, I'm just kidding. Occasionally, it was Fox Sports.

November 14, 2009
2:44 am

This just in... Beer is good.

November 16, 2009
5:33 pm

Jack's starting to make more eye contact. Not only are his eyes bigger and more full of life, but he's starting to look at us as if he's realizes that he's a person and so are we. He's still crying as much as ever, but now when he does, he looks at us pleadingly as if to say, "Help me."

As a result, he's started to tug at our hearts even more. It's as if he doesn't particularly want to cry and fidget and make our lives hell, but he just can't help it.

Sometimes, he even uses his eyes to smile. On "America's Next Top Model," which Preva watches too frequently for me not to pick up the occasional phrase, they call smiling with your eyes "smize-ing." Jack's been smize-ing lately and it's pretty awesome.

November 17, 2009
10:05 pm

Last night was Jack's first night in his big boy crib.

Up until last night, Jack was sleeping in our bedroom with Preva and I've been staying in the guest room to try and get as much sleep as I can. See, she's a great sleeper and I'm the opposite.

If a ceiling fan hums too loudly or if a cat starts snoring or the temperature in the room rises to 74 1/2 degrees from its pre-set 74, I tend to have trouble falling asleep.

It's a bone of contention for Preva. Okay, it's more like an entire skeleton of contention for her. But since that's probably the biggest problem in our marriage, she doesn't complain too much.

Anyway, that's why there was little chance I'd be able to doze off, what with Jack's constant grunting combined with the television blasting, which Preva employs to muffle the grunting.

We were told that infants can be in their own room at between six and eight weeks of age, so we felt it was time for such a move.

Jack doesn't squirm around too much in his sleep, so that combined with the "wedge" pillow which keeps him from turning over, makes us more confident that he won't end up in a position where he'll have trouble breathing.

Plus, once he's asleep (which still doesn't happen until one or two a.m.), he now stays asleep for four-plus hours rather than the three-plus hours he did during the first six weeks of his life.

I was giddy at the notion of sharing a bed with my wife for the first time since Jack was born. Not because I thought anything would happen along the lines of what occasionally happens in bed between a man and wife who love each other very much, mind you. Both of us are too tired and one of us still feels too "unsexy" after giving birth.

I just wanted to be able to sleep next to my wife while spooning our dogs. That was my old, comfortable routine before my new, uncomfortable routine took over.

So, around 1:00 am, we finished giving Jack his bottle, soothed him to sleepydom, and put him in his crib. He glanced around thoughtfully at his new surroundings as if he appreciated the change in scenery.

I couldn't believe how tiny he looked. He looked like a grain of rice in a gravy boat. He looked like the Olson twins in a Hummer. He seemed too small to be in his own room, but experience and our doctors' advice assuaged our fears.

I backed slowly out of the room, hoping against hope he might actually fall asleep without crying.

But right before I shut the door, it started. And it was impressive. This crying fit gave all of his other crying fits a run for their money. Preva and I laid in bed, watching him cry on the baby monitor, and listening to his deafening wails of displeasure. It was so loud and angry, it sounded like an entire theater full of film critics screening the newest Vin Diesel movie.

Our doctor told us that babies are fine to scream their brains out for up to twenty minutes before you should make sure that something isn't wrong.

Preva, being the softie in the crying department, wanted to go get him. But sure enough, at the twenty-minute mark, the crying stopped. He was out.

Julia was in her room, Jack was in his room, and we were in ours. The way it should be. We smiled and held each other while we watched an old episode of "Entourage" and drifted off to sleep.

If Jack would do this every night at 9:30 pm instead of 1:30 am, this could be our new nightly routine. But his body clock hasn't turned around enough for that to be possible. And Preva needs her rest too much for me to let him cry himself to sleep.

She went through so much with pregnancy and giving birth and resisting the urge to kill me when the seamstress I convinced her to go with screwed up the alterations on her wedding dress and she nearly tripped over it several times while walking down the aisle, and to this day she won't watch our wedding video because of it, even though it really was a lovely occasion in spite of the wildfires that caused all of our guests to be stuck in traffic for three hours, severely shortening the reception... that the least I can do is exhaust myself to the brink of collapse to make sure she gets her rest.

November 18, 2009
12:32 pm

In case you can't tell, I don't just love my wife. I like her more than anyone I've ever known. Because she's the kindest, funniest, most caring person I've ever known.

It's impossible not to like her, and if you don't, then you need to have your head examined. If everything checks out with your head, then have your heart examined, because if you do, I'm guessing you'll find that you don't even have one.

She's such a warm and personable person (despite her occasional potty mouth and readiness to tell me when I've screwed up) that complete strangers often end up telling her their life story within two minutes of meeting her.

This morning, we were running errands while Jack was screaming in the backseat. We stopped at the dry cleaners and Preva ran inside. I continued driving around the block to try and get Jack to nod off.

When I returned, Preva still hadn't come out yet. I took another lap, but she still wasn't out. I tried calling her, but she didn't answer her phone. I called again. Fifteen minutes passed and there was still no sign of her.

Finally, I parked, took our screaming son out of the car, and entered the dry cleaners. Preva wasn't there. I described her to the woman behind the counter, who said that she'd taken her dry cleaning and left. I was worried and confused. Where could she be?

I left the dry cleaners. Out of the corner of my eye, I saw her in Starbucks with a woman I didn't know. The woman looked distraught. Preva was nodding and holding her hand. I smiled. I'd seen this kind of thing before.

I walked back to the car with Jack who was finally asleep. A few minutes later, Preva emerged from Starbucks. I flagged her down and she hopped in.

She explained that the woman had been in the dry cleaners and Preva had asked what was wrong. She was recently divorced and was having trouble dealing with it.

For the next ten minutes, she listened to this complete stranger spill her guts to her, and by the end of it, my amazing wife had the woman laughing and realizing that she was better off "without that schmuck."

It's amazing, but Preva has that effect on everyone she meets. Everyone except Jack, of course.

Out of the approximately 5,000 "take a picture of ourselves while holding the camera" pictures we've taken, this is the only decent shot.

November 18, 2009
10:35 pm

What the *&^#$(#$&* is up with those *&^#$(#$&* side-by-side strollers?! Not all of them. But the really big ones. You know the ones.

Why exactly do parents think it's okay to push around those obnoxiously wide strollers that take up an entire shopping aisle?!

I don't care if you have twins or if you think that a regular double stroller makes the kid sitting in back feel inferior like it might hamper his psychological or emotional development. They're rude, ridiculous, and unnecessary.

There's a reason why people don't usually walk around town wildly swinging ski poles or pushing hospital gurneys turned sideways. It tends to impede the progress of those walking in the opposite direction.

So, just say "no" to those stupid *&^#$(#$&* baby zamboni's. There. I feel better.

November 19, 2009
8:44 am

I've heard that the definition of "insanity" is doing the same thing over and over and hoping for different results. In our house, the definition of insanity is the hours between eight p.m. and two a.m. when Jack is going full throttle and nothing seems to soothe him.

Trying to avoid the first definition, last night I decided to try something different to soothe the unsoothable. I decided to give the "miracle blanket" another shot.

For the uninitiated, the "miracle blanket" is a swaddle that more effectively prevents a baby's arms and legs from moving. It's essentially a straitjacket for newborns, although lately, Preva and I are the ones who need the straitjacket.

Babies find the confinement comforting because it reminds them of being in the womb. And being unable to move their arms means that they don't flail about or whack themselves in the head when they're asleep. Thus, once they *do* fall asleep, they stay asleep much longer.

It worked great with Julia, but naturally, with Jack it didn't take. We put him in it the first night we brought him home, but he screamed for an hour until we took him out of it. We tried again the next night, but he screamed even louder for even longer. Almost fool him once, shame on us. Almost fool him twice, shame on us even more.

But last night, as I was dizzy and hunched over in pain from walking in circles with Jack in my arms for the past forty minutes, I spotted the miracle blanket crumpled up in the corner of my office. Figuring I had nothing to lose, I laid Jack on the bed, and wrapped him up tightly in it.

As soon as I did, his face relaxed and his crying stopped. Jack laid there silently for ten minutes before closing his eyes. And just like that, he was asleep. I couldn't believe it. Maybe six days was too young for the miracle blanket, but now that he was six weeks, his body and mind were mature enough to let the garment work its alleged magic.

I high-fived myself, I fist-bumped myself, and I would have patted myself on the back, except that after a month-and-a-half of holding Jack, my arms no longer bend that way.

It was sheer and unadulterated bliss. And it lasted for exactly three-and-a-half minutes. At that point, Jack opened his eyes and was back in "full bawl" mode before I knew what hit me.

I tried the so-called miracle blanket twenty minutes later and then another twenty minutes after that. It didn't work either time.

With Jack, we need more than a miracle. We should have known that even if this garment delivered what it promised, it wouldn't be enough.

November 22, 2009
12:33 am

Until Jack came along, I never drank coffee. I didn't need to. I never liked the taste and I always took a certain amount of pride in not being a slave to it like practically everyone else I know. I also enjoyed the look of shock on peoples' faces when they would say, "You don't drink coffee?" as if I'd discovered the mythical Fountain of Alertness and wasn't telling anyone about it.

Unfortunately, Jack has turned me into a coffee drinker. I've spent countless days in Starbucks over the years, since it's the perfect place to write. But now I find myself going there simply to buy coffee. Iced venti nonfat lattes, to be painfully specific.

It's so pretentious-sounding that I've considered putting on a bank robber's mask, writing down my order on a slip of paper, and sliding it across the counter to the barista like a holdup note.

I hate that I've become one of those people who orders a beverage that takes longer to say than it does to drink, but I have and it's all because of Jack. That's why I blame him for what happened this morning.

I walked into my local Starbucks and saw a female barista behind the counter. She was probably in college. Or high school. Or elementary school. Or maybe she was thirty. I just didn't know, because I'm now old enough to be one of those people who has no idea how old anyone is.

Anyway, I happened to notice that she had a nametag on her apron that read "Tina."

I'm not the kind who usually addresses people by their name if I don't know them, but this time -- and probably for the last time -- I did.

"Hello, Tina!" I said. "How's it going today?"

She raised an eyebrow. "Do I know you?"

"No," I said. "I just saw your name on your apron."

"Oh," Tina replied, smiling. "I thought maybe you were a friend of my mom's or something."

Her mom?! I immediately went numb. At that moment, she could have thrown a pot of hot coffee in my face, poked me in the eye with a scone, or sliced my throat with a Starbucks holiday CD featuring artists like U2 and John Legend, and I wouldn't have felt it.

My face dropped. After I finished lifting my jaw out of the tip jar and scraped the loose change off my chin, I looked at her and mustered a very weak and a very unmanly, "Your mom?"

"Yeah," she replied, completely unaware of where my hurt or confusion might be stemming from.

"Is your mom thirty?" I asked hopefully.

"No, she forty-seven," she replied matter-of-factly.

I nodded and looked up at the menu, even though I already knew what I was ordering. At that point, a lightbulb went off in her head, a head which could have been anywhere from 12 to 30 years old.

"I'm not saying you look old, I just..." she started. I stopped her right there.

"It's okay," I said. "I am old. And tired. And I really need a venti iced nonfat latte."

"I drink those," she said, smiling.

I don't know if she was just saying that to make me feel better, but it did. For a minute, I didn't feel quite so old. And then I ordered a bran muffin, because I could use the fiber.

Preva's parents.
They both just turned… 35, I think?

November 23, 2009
5:52 pm

It was a valiant effort at any rate.

Jack had been asleep for twenty minutes and based on recent napping history, I was pretty sure he'd be asleep for at least another half an hour. We needed to pick Julia up from school at 4:00.

Anyway, Preva and I haven't done that thing that grown-up's do who love each other very much since Jack was born and I'm starting to get a little… antsy. The doctor told her that she wasn't allowed to until the six-week mark and it's now almost eight weeks.

Since we're both always tired and she's not even close to letting me see her naked yet, I'm not sure there is such thing as a "good time." Nevertheless, this time seemed as "un-bad" as any.

I heard Preva walking down the stairs, so I quickly started walking up. I blocked her path, with her standing one stair higher than me. This was a calculated maneuver on my part, because ever since we started dating and we found ourselves on an escalator, she would stand one stair higher than me so that our faces were even and kiss me.

I hugged her. She smiled and I squeezed her tight as I sweetly whispered in her ear.

ME: "Do you want to... you know?"
PREVA: "Nuh-uh."
ME: "Just real quick?"
PREVA: "Nope."
ME: "I need to feel close to you."
PREVA: "Please go empty the diaper pail. It stinks."

I nodded and stepped aside as she continued down the stairs. I thought for a minute before asking, "Did I almost have you with the 'need to feel close to you' thing?"

"Sorry. Not even a little."

However, after she said that, she gave a slight smirk, which let me know that she didn't blame me for trying. She might have even appreciated it.

"I didn't mean right here on the stairs," I yelled, as she disappeared into the kitchen.

November 24, 2009
11:00 am

Last night's shower was pretty much like all the others before it. I soaped and rinsed Jack clean before staring into his eyes for at least ten minutes as I psychically pleaded for a breakthrough in his overall disposition.

Needless to say, it didn't take. As soon as I turned off the water and handed him to Preva, he resumed crying. But on a scale of 1 to 10, this crying was a "74."

We did our usual shower switch, with Julia getting into the shower and the boys getting out. Preva wrapped the now screaming Jack in his towel, laid him on the bed, and went to get his jammies. As Jack kept screaming, I started combing my hair.

"Could you please pick him up?!" Preva yelled from the other room.

I dropped what I was doing and went to grab him. I don't have scientific data to back this up, but I think the average parent "drops what he's doing" approximately 572 times a day.

While I ran into the bedroom, my towel fell to the floor, leaving me naked as a jaybird, which for whatever reason is the nakedest bird in all of nature.

Preva tossed Jack's jammies onto the bed while she went in to make sure that Julia wasn't showering the entire bathroom with the hand sprayer. I quickly jammied Jack and his screaming subsided ever so slightly. At this point, Preva re-entered the bedroom, grabbed a pair of my boxers, and walked toward me.

I smiled as she knelt down to help me put on my boxers. She's a great wife and never is it more apparent than moments like this, with her nose inches away from

Erik Jr. I laughed as she shook her head like "I can't believe I'm doing this." Unfortunately, the humor of the moment was short-lived.

I lifted my right leg to step into the boxers. At that moment, Jack resumed his crying and I turned my head to "shush" him. However, I continued raising my leg and my knee hit Preva right in the forehead. Hard.

Preva dropped my boxers, put her hand to her forehead, and yelled something that isn't normally yelled in our house. But alas, here it was, as loud and as robust any curse word has ever been uttered. She opened her mouth and yelled "FUUUUUUUUCK!"

Jack stopped crying, our two pit bulls slinked out of the room, and from the bathroom, we heard a very clear, a very calm, and -- dare I say, a very cute -- "Fuck."

I started laughing. Preva shot me a look. It was a new record. I had now done two very wrong things in just under four seconds.

We all marched into the bathroom to find Julia amusing herself with her suction cup fish as if nothing had happened.

"What did you say?" I asked, secretly hoping she would say it again.

"Fuck," she replied, before adding, "Mommy, can I use your toothbrush?"

I laughed again. I couldn't help it. I'd never heard the F-bomb detonated so cutely and so innocently, and I loved the way it echoed in our bathroom.

Preva shot me another look, but by now her pain had subsided enough for her to realize how, well, fucking funny it was. She covered her face with her hand so that Julia couldn't see her laughing.

She gathered herself and looked at Julia. "Honey, I don't want you saying that word."

"What wrong with 'toothbrush'?" Julia responded.

Preva continued laughing and looked at me for help.

"What?" I asked.

"This is your fault!" she said.

"What?! I'm not the one who said the 'f' word!"

She shot me a look, her face a fascinating mix of anger and amusement. I looked at Julia and said, "Honey, don't say 'fuck.' That's a grown-up word."

"Oh. Like 'crap'?"

Preva and I looked at each other.

"Where did you hear 'crap'?" I asked. She shrugged her shoulders.

"Did you hear Pierce or Lukas or Kaden or Kory say it?" we asked, wondering if she would throw her friends under the bus. She shook her head.

"Did you hear it at school?" I asked.

"Well, no," Julia answered.

"Hell no?!" Preva responded.

"Relax," I said, laughing. "She said, '*Well*, no'."

"Oh," Preva said, relieved.

Still, did we curse more than we thought? Was Julia sneaking out of her room and watching Quentin Tarantino movies while we were asleep? Would Jack soon turn into the same adorably potty-mouthed toddler that Julia had become? We just didn't know.

"Julia, I don't want to hear you say those words again," I said.

Julia understood that what she'd said was wrong. We, too, were satisfied that a lesson had been learned. Then again, if it hadn't, we were frankly too tired to care.

For now, we have bigger, crankier fish to fry.

At the First Annual "Parents of Newborns Who Pretend to be Rested and Happy Picnic."

November 24, 2009
8:43 pm

I could be sitting on the couch eating sushi and watching the "Sopranos" on DVD like I always said I would. But I'm not. Instead, I'm cleaning puke off the carpet because after ten minutes of trying to burp Jack, he finally decided he'd rather just puke.

This is what I've chosen. I won't lie. It's a process.

November 24, 2009
11:33 pm

As a parent, it's incredible the highs and lows you experience on a daily basis.

One minute, you're having this conversation at the dinner table:

ME: "Julia, please eat your macaroni."
JULIA: "I'm full."
PREVA: "If she's full, that's fine. But no dessert."
ME: "She's *not* full and when we put her to bed, she's going to yell for an hour about being hungry until you bring her a banana!"
PREVA: "A banana's not dessert!"
ME: "I know, but she'd rather have a banana than macaroni!"
PREVA: "Bananas are good for you. They have potassium!"
ME: "Well, macaroni has protein!"
PREVA: "Protein?"
ME: "Yeah, 'cause of the cheese!"
PREVA: "Not the instant kind!"
ME: "Does, too!"
PREVA: "What are you, 'Dr. Macaroni'?!"
ME: "No, I'm 'Dr. Pasta'. But I specialize in macaroni."
PREVA: "Shut up."
ME: "Get the box. Let's check."
PREVA: "I'm not checking the box to see if the cheese in instant macaroni has protein! I'm just so tired of begging her to eat!"
ME: "Is that my fault?"
PREVA: "Yes, because your side of the family is a bunch of skinny people who don't care about food!"
ME: "We like food. We just don't start planning Thanksgiving dinner in February like your family does!"

And with that, dinner abruptly ends. Preva goes up to her room to decompress by watching "Top Chef," while I give Julia a banana and some ice cream (nutrition and dessert in one fell swoop), so that I can finish my work and be in bed by ten o'clock.

From here on, you probably know the drill. You figure you and your wife will spend the rest of the night tiptoeing around each other, wondering who will bite the bullet and apologize to the other first.

However, just an hour later, when you're putting your daughter to bed, you have this conversation:

ME: "Good night, Julia."
JULIA: "I'm so glad you're my daddy."
ME: "I'm so glad you're my daughter. I love you so much."
As I start to shut the door...
JULIA: "Daddy?"
ME: "Yes, honey?"
JULIA: "I love you so much, it hurts my heart."
ME: "What did you say?"
JULIA: "I love you so much, it hurts my heart. I want to live with you forever."
ME: "I hope you still feel that way in twenty years when some loser with no job asks you to move in with him."
JULIA: "What?"
ME: "Nothing. I love you so much, sweetie."
JULIA: "I love you, daddy. Go tell mommy to come kiss me and say goodnight."

I shut the door as I start choking up. I walk into our bedroom to find Preva, whom I haven't spoken to in an hour, watching the conclusion of her show. She knows I'm there, but doesn't look up.

ME: "Honey, can I tell you something?"
PREVA: "Let me guess. Instant macaroni has protein?"

ME: "No, it's something that Julia just said."
Preva sighs as she pushes "pause" and looks at me.
PREVA: "What?"
ME: "Julia just said that she loves me so much, it hurts her heart."
PREVA: (melting) "Ohhhh... You're kidding..."

I walk over to the bed and we hug in a way that lets each of us know that the other is sorry for the way that dinner ended. It's also a hug that says, "I love you," "We're so lucky," and "There's nobody I'd want to change places with."

When we became parents, we found ourselves going from arguing about something stupid and wanting to abandon Julia at a Chuck E. Cheese to realizing that she's the most amazing kid in the universe before we even knew what hit us.

And that was BEFORE Jack was born.

That was *before* I had to try and make a living writing comedy on five hours of sleep, *before* Preva had to walk around all day with boobs that smell like curdled milk, and *before* we had to make sure that our three-year-old never felt like she was taking a backseat to the brother she now shares a backseat with.

Now that Jack's here, we're getting less sleep, we have less patience, and there's less time to get everything done.

Yet somehow, there's even more love in our house, there are even more things that make us laugh, and we have even more reminders of just how fortunate we are.

That means the highs are even higher, the lows are even lower, and we alternate back and forth between the two faster than the speed of light.

And nothing is faster than the speed of light. Except maybe the rate at which Jack goes from being sound asleep to screaming loud enough to wake the neighbors. Our old neighbors. The ones who live ten miles away.

If you ever find yourself holding a hammer,
a light saber, and a Mike's Hard Lemonade…
then you're probably a dad.

November 26, 2009
3:02 am

This just in… Beer is *still* good. Necessary, even.

November 26, 2009
11:22 pm

Tonight we hosted our first Thanksgiving. Jack took the opportunity to prove that it's true what they say. Kids never perform when you want them to. And certainly not our Jack, who turned two months old today.

Even though our friends and relatives have heard about how hard Jack's been, we try not to be the kind of parents who constantly whine about how hard infants are. Because complaining about babies being a lot of work is like going to Disneyland and complaining about how long the lines are. It's annoying and everyone pretty much already knows anyway.

We started eating around four, and from then until around nine o'clock when people started leaving, Jack was pleasant if not downright adorable.

He usually starts ratcheting up the crankiness at around seven, but tonight he actually became mellower. He even smiled a few times as relatives passed him around like a dish of creamed corn that nobody wanted. No one said anything, but I knew what they were thinking:

"This is the colicky baby you've been talking about? You two must be the problem, because this child puts the 'd' in 'delightful'!"

In order for people to get a glimpse of the real Jack, I was tempted to pinch his foot or pour cranberry sauce over his head or tell him that we'd have so many leftovers he'd be eating turkey sandwiches well into his teens, but I didn't.

We had a fun day with lots of good food, and about ten minutes after everyone left, Jack started crying. Both Preva's and my parents were the only four people who witnessed the amazing transformation from dream baby to nightmare infant of the apocalypse.

At our first Thanksgiving, our relatives were fooled into thinking that Jack is just another baby who simply gets a little cranky at times. Granted, it's not as tragic as the very *first* Thanksgiving when the Indians were fooled into thinking that the white man was their friend. But it's a shame nonetheless.

At least I'll have plenty of wine and stuffing to tide me over for the next three hours until Jack falls asleep.

November 27, 2009
10:15 am

In spite of the wine and the leftovers, last night was another long, physically and emotionally draining night. I'm tired and bitter that Jack hasn't turned the corner and shows no intention of doing so. But at least I'm not Tiger Woods.

I just heard on the news that he backed his SUV into a tree and a fire hydrant at the end of his driveway last night at two o'clock in the morning. Seems very un-Tiger-like. I have a feeling this won't be the last we'll be hearing about this.

Am I allowed to re-gift my son?

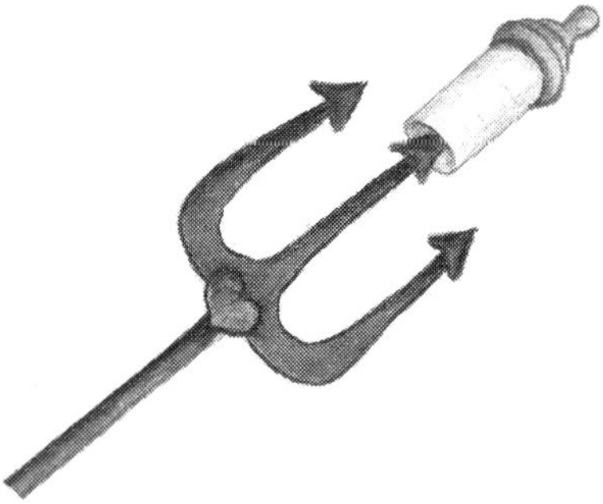

MONTH THREE

November 27, 2009
3:14 pm

Many years ago, Preva and I made a choice at the deli counter of life. We don't even remember walking into the deli, but we must have. All couples do.

We entered the deli and took a number. We looked at the menu above the counter, which listed only one entree.

This was the entree's description:

"A life where you have less free time and even less disposable income, in which your patience will be tested each and every day. You'll wake up early, always be in a hurry, worry more, and relax less. You'll feel overworked, underappreciated, and there's a chance you'll never be able to retire. If you do retire, instead of it being to a house within walking distance of the beach, it will be to a condo within biking distance of an Arby's."

We looked at each other. It didn't sound that appetizing, but we'd both always wanted kids. Plus, it was the only thing on the menu, so naturally, that's what we'd be ordering. But then, something caught our eye.

We noticed a small dry-erase board on the wall next to the cash register. An employee with obvious artistic talent had drawn lots of beautiful flowers and birds and other eye-catching objects around the board's border in bright, carefully chosen colors.

Inside the border, the employee had written, "TODAY'S SPECIAL," which was this:

"A fun, relatively carefree existence where you can do what you want and have plenty of money to do it. An existence in which you can retire early, give more money to charity, travel the world, and fall asleep while reading a book without worrying about being woken up by screaming, crying, or someone jumping on your bed yelling, 'I gotta go poo'!"

Preva and I looked at each other again. The Special sounded pretty good. Suddenly, we weren't so sure about our order.

Then we heard the door "jingle." We turned and saw a thirty-five-year-old man and his six-year-old son enter the deli.

"Why didn't you go before we left home?!" the dad angrily asked his son.

"I didn't have to go then," the boy replied, tears streaming down his cheeks.

"I'm so tired of you doing this. I just don't understand," the dad said, shaking his head, as they marched toward the bathroom.

"Don't be mad," the boy pleaded.

"I'm not mad. Just disappointed," the exasperated dad said, which really seemed to sting the boy. "One day, you'll start listening," he added as they disappeared into the bathroom.

Suddenly, the Special sounded even more appetizing than ever. Preva and I studied the two menu choices as we stepped aside and let several other people order ahead of us.

Just then, we heard the bathroom door open. We all turned to see if the father and son had reached some sort of post-tinkle truce.

But instead of seeing the same thirty-five-year-old dad and six-year-old son who had entered the bathroom, we saw a sixty-five-year-old man and a thirty-six-year-old man.

The older man looked like an older version of the dad who had entered the bathroom. The younger man had the same brown eyes and sandy blond hair as the boy. We then realized that they were the same two people, just thirty years older.

Instead of crying, the son was now laughing. "Can't wait 'til we get to the golf course?" he asked his dad, playfully punching him in the arm.

"It's your fault," he replied. "You know I can't have two cups of coffee."

The son smiled and said, "I told you not to have that second cup. One day you'll start listening." The dad laughed.

"It's good to see you," the son continued.

"You know we drive up to see you every chance we get," the dad replied. "It all just goes way too fast."

"I know," the son said.

With that, the father and son opened the door and exited the deli.

"What do you want to get?" Preva asked.

"I don't know. What do <u>you</u> want to get?" I responded.

The girl behind the counter said, "Fifty-seven!"

We looked down at our ticket. That was our number. We walked to the counter. I held Preva's hand. She squeezed it tight as she took a deep breath, smiled, and said, "We'll have the 'number one'."

"You don't want the Special?" the girl asked, surprised.

"No thanks," I said.

"Are you sure? It comes with fries," she added.

"Curly or regular?" I asked as Preva punched me in the arm.

"We'll have the number one," I said. We then went and sat down while we waited for our order to be ready.

November 28, 2009
8:44 pm

It recently occurred to me that babies are like cigarettes. They're little, they're expensive, they smell bad, they annoy people in public places, they should be illegal on airplanes, and nobody under 21 should be allowed to have one.

There are differences, however. Cigarettes make you lose weight, while babies make you lose sleep. Cigarettes make you live shorter lives, while babies make you live longer, more fulfilling lives.

At the end of every parent's life, he thinks, "I'm sure glad I had kids." At the end of every smoker's life, he thinks, "No wonder nobody ever wanted to ride in my car."

November 29, 2009
8:31 pm

I really, really didn't want to wash bottles today.

I was standing at the sink, waiting for the water to get hot enough to kill whatever deadly germs can emanate from crusty breast milk when Preva walked up behind me.

"It's warm enough," she said, testing the water coming out of the tap. I didn't answer. I just stared in a daze at all the dirty, nauseatingly foul-smelling bottles in the sink.

"Honey?" she asked. "You okay?"

"I don't want to wash bottles," I said, finally summoning the strength to speak. "I'm so tired of it."

"Oh, really? You're 'tired' of it? That's fascinating, because I'm tired of *everything*."

With that, the nosiest three-year-old in the world poked her head out of her room.

JULIA: "What's going on?"
PREVA: "Daddy won't wash bottles."
ERIK: "I want mommy to do it."
JULIA: "Whose turn is it?"
PREVA: "It's daddy's turn."
ERIK: "Why?"
PREVA: "Because it is. I wash *twice* as many bottles as you. It's your turn. Go."
ERIK: "Let's just buy new bottles."
PREVA: "You still have to boil them."
ERIK: "Perfect. It's your turn to boil bottles."
PREVA: "Erik!"
JULIA: "Okay, daddy, how about this?"
ERIK: "How about what?"

JULIA: "How about if I sing and dance to make you happy while you wash bottles?"
ERIK: "Hmm... But you sing and dance all the time anyway. It almost seems like that might be more fun for you than for me."
JULIA: "Here goes!"

And with that, Julia starts to sing and dance, as we both start laughing.

I proceed to wash bottles and Preva feeds Jack. It's nine o'clock and the hardest five hours are still to come.

"Watch me... all the time!"

November 30, 2009
9:30 pm

I don't know what Preva would do if she didn't have Bentley to spoon with in bed at the end of a long day. That dog has almost singlehandedly gotten her through two very rough pregnancies, one stressful move, and now Jack.

Somehow, she knows when Preva needs extra love, comfort, and affection even more than I do.

We both love that girl with the huge head and soulful brown eyes way too much. More than we should. It's not healthy. But it can't be helped.

November 30, 2009
11:54 pm

I won't mention the name of Preva's favorite restaurant, but it's a certain pizza kitchen that originated in California. To her great delight, one of these California-based kitchens specializing in pizza recently opened up about three miles from our house.

It's the talk of the town and there's always at least an hour wait, which is why we usually do take-out. However, Preva had a rough day (a.k.a. "a perfectly normal day with a colicky newborn"), so tonight we decided to get out of the house and "dine in" along with every other person in Valencia.

There were two small problems (major tragedies) with our dining experience (dinner from hell.)

The first problem is that this particular kitchen for making California-style pizzas, which obviously shall remain nameless, recently started printing the calorie count for each item on their menu, making it impossible to eat a certain item without thinking about how many 10K marathons you need to run to burn it off.

You don't tell a new mom with thirty pounds to lose that her favorite salad is 1,200 calories. You just don't do it.

"This is so stupid!" Preva said, tears welling up in her eyes.

I agreed, but was still dumb enough to say, "Honey, it doesn't matter. You still need to order your favorite salad. You *deserve* it."

"I don't deserve to be told how much fatter I'm gonna get!" she said, pushing the menu away. "This salad has more than a thousand calories! Let's go!"

"You don't have to put dressing on it," I offered. She said nothing, but gave me an icy stare that told me, "You're not a salad guy. Please shut up."

Being similarly affected by the in-your-face calorie counts, I decided to have fish since it was the healthiest thing on the menu. I suggested she do the same.

"Fine," she said, slamming a red crayon down onto a drawing of an apple on the kids' menu. At least she had the right color.

When the waitress arrived, I ordered my fish "blackened," but gave explicit instructions that Preva's wasn't to be blackened. She simply can't handle spice or Cajun-inspired excitement of any kind.

The waitress said she understood. She looked like she understood. She said, "I got it." She nodded. She wrote things down. She promised she would tell the chef.

Over the next fifteen minutes, both of our moods improved. Jack was sleeping. We were laughing. Everything was great. Then the food came.

The waitress handed Julia her meal and then put our plates down in front of us.

Here's where that second problem comes in.

Preva looked down at her piece of fish, which, like my piece of fish, was as black as her mood was about to become.

"We told you not... You said you weren't... This fish is..." she stammered, unable to sufficiently express all of the thoughts in her angry little head.

"It's blackened," I said to the waitress, shaking my head.

"You blackened it!" Preva yelled, loudly enough for everyone at the surrounding tables to hear. I cringed.

Since the waitress was African-American, I was hoping they heard *exactly* what Preva said rather than thinking she was hurling a racial insult of some kind.

"I'm so sorry," the waitress said, reaching for her plate. "I'll bring you another meal."

"That's okay," I replied. "We don't have time. We'll just scrape off the black part.

Read the shirt.
It's (kind of) funny because it's true.

I felt a little bad for her. It was probably the chef's screw-up. But if you screw up the order of the parent of a colicky baby and don't end up with your eye being gouged out with a pacifier (because we have no other use for it), you're getting off easy.

As I started to scrape off the unwanted char, Preva shook her head, "I'll just eat the veggies."

It could have been so different. If the menu hadn't listed the calories, I would have had pizza, she would have had her beloved salad, and everything would have been great. But that didn't happen.

"I'm sorry," I finally said, hoping for a smile of some kind.

"I hate my life," she replied, a piece of broccoli hanging out of the side of her mouth.

December 2, 2009
1:41 am

I keep hoping it's true that colic can literally end "overnight." Can that really be true? Can the baby of my nightmares really turn into the baby of my dreams "just like that"? As he approaches the three-month mark, I just don't see how that's possible.

For the most part, he's just as bad as ever. But if it somehow ended after three months, it would be the best Christmas present I could possibly receive. I would never ask for or expect anything else for the rest of my life. But I'm not getting my hopes up.

December 2, 2009
6:12 pm

Okay, this is getting good. Really good. Turns out, Tiger Woods has been having an affair for almost three years with some cute-in-a-skanky-way cocktail waitress, including during the time when his wife Elin was pregnant.

People are speculating that she was chasing him down the driveway with a golf club, which is why he crashed.

I think the moral in all of this is, if you're a dad, you should be too busy working or helping with the kids or spending every waking minute telling your pregnant wife "Thank you, thank you, thank you for everything you're going through" to have an affair.

Either that or "Get a shorter driveway" so that you can back out of it faster to get away from your golf club-wielding wife.

When I asked Preva if she would come after me with a golf club if I had an affair, she said, "Of course. But if you made $50 million a year, I'd let you tell me where you wanted me to hit you."

December 3, 2009
8:42 pm

Today, I was so tired that I nearly fell asleep while standing at a urinal.

December 3, 2009
10:24 pm

I love working on "America's Funniest Home Videos" largely because of how much joy it brings to so many millions of people. There aren't many shows that the entire family can watch together that can keep everyone laughing for an entire hour.

Whether we're writing jokes to accompany the videos or just deciding which videos are funny enough to make the show, we literally spend all day watching TV. I know. Poor us.

But the job's a lot more challenging than that. We also spend a lot of time arguing about what we should order for lunch. To be honest, all TV writers are basically big, coffee-powered babies who only think about food.

There are a lot of people who have worked on the show during its twenty years on the air, but almost all of the credit for its success goes to one man, its creator Vin Di Bona. Not only is he a very funny and generous man, but he knows how to construct each show so that it has the perfect blend of funny, cute, and "I'm glad that's his crotch and not mine."

Having a family isn't easy. But as I sit in the office watching videos of other families laughing, playing jokes on each other, and finding humor in the millions of little moments that make up a day, I'm constantly reminded of just how funny and rewarding it is.

The good news is that Jack will soon be just as entertaining as the kids I spend all day watching at work. The bad news is that even if I capture it on video and get it on the show, I won't be eligible to win the $100,000 prize.

December 6, 2009
1:19 am

I just put Jack to bed with the same nighttime lullaby CD that we've been using since Julia was a baby.

That means we've been listening to the same CD with the same twenty-four songs for more than three years, which is well over a thousand straight nights.

The only way to make the songs tolerable is to make up my own lyrics while I'm trying to calm Jack down enough to put in his crib. Singing helps drown out his wailing as well as distract myself from my own aching shoulders, knees, and back.

The only I song that I truly despise is "Mockingbird." I have real problems with that song.

Not only is it the most annoying and the most monotonous tune, but it also makes zero sense. There's not a mom alive who would buy her baby a mockingbird, a billy goat, *and* a diamond ring.

Except maybe Celine Dion. For some reason, I can see her doing that. It wouldn't even have to be the kid's birthday.

Also, can a person return a mockingbird simply because it doesn't sing? Even if you keep the receipt, I can see you having to jump through a lot of hoops to convince them to take it back.

"Mockingbird" is song number five on the CD. I always try to get out of the room before that one starts playing. When I can't, I'm forced to improvise in order to stay sane. I did again tonight.

Hush, little baby, don't say a word
Mama's gonna buy you a mockingbird

As soon as I start singing, Jack was silent, probably wondering why for the first time all day I was singing instead of yell-whispering "SHHHHHH!" until my throat's raw.

And if that mockingbird won't sing
Jay-Z's gonna go buy himself some bling

Jack either hated my singing or Jay-Z references because he promptly resumed his crying.

And if Jay-Z's bling is stolen by his posse
Alyssa Milano starred in "Who's the Boss-y?"

We were now in competition, with Jack crying even louder to make sure that he was heard.

"Who's the Boss" wasn't a great show
Preva has a freakishly long second toe

I started using Jack's hand like a microphone since his arm is the same length as a microphone and his fist is the same size and shape as the end.

Her second toe is long, 'cause her big toe was shortened
In a bunion-removal procedure, but that's not important

In fact, I could paint his arm black and put a black foam microphone cover over the end to really make it complete. Who am I kidding? I would never go through the trouble of actually doing that.

She got pissed at the doc and her bitterness lingers
Her toe's the same length and shape of E.T.'s finger

Jack's crying changed pitch almost as if he was trying to harmonize with me.

Before I met Preva, I didn't know from bunions
I'm getting kind of hungry, I hope we have Funyuns

And just like that, Jack fell asleep.

It was easy tonight. I got lucky. Things are very slowly getting better. As long as there's progress being made -- however painfully gradual it may be -- we're able to see that there might actually be a nightlight at the end of the tunnel.

I'm about 99% sure that I could feed Jack to this elephant and nobody would ever know.

December 7, 2009
11:19 pm

During his nap, Jack took perhaps the biggest dump of his life -- or of any Lohla's life, for that matter -- with 20% staying in his diaper and the 80% somehow winding up on his back.

Most people will remember December 7th for the attack on Pearl Harbor. I'll remember it for Jack's dump.

Said dump must have occurred toward the beginning of his nap, because by the time he woke up, it was as hard and as black as the La Brea Tar Pits. Except that Jack's dump would probably be more interesting to visit than the La Brea Tar Pits. Plus, it's open on Mondays.

When we can, Preva and I tag-team Jack's poops, employing a division of labor technique that shortens the process and benefits everyone involved. However, Preva was napping when Jack woke up, so I had to attack this poop solo.

It's pointless to tell a friend who doesn't have kids (or someone whose kids are older and has forgotten how grim it can be) about having to change a really gnarly diaper. Your story will either bore or gross them out. And even if you go into detail, which they don't appreciate, it never really captures just how involved the process is.

Thus, I've broken down the steps of changing this particularly nasty diaper into numbered steps:

1) Lift Jack out of his crib and place him onto his changing table without gagging.
2) Quickly run out of his room into the hallway to take a huge breath so that I don't have to inhale for the next two-and-a-half-minutes.

3) Unzip Jack's pajamas, which are stuck to his back with the amazing adhesive "Super Poo."
4) Turn Jack on his side in an attempt to separate him from his pajamas by holding his arm in one hand and the pajamas in other and yanking in opposite directions.
5) Realize that, while separating Jack from his pajamas, he's reached down with his free arm and gotten a handful of poop, which has also squirted out the *front* of his diaper.
6) Quickly toss the dirty pajamas aside while I grab a baby wipe to clean Jack's dirty hand before he puts it in his mouth.
7) Wipe his hand and then clean poop off his stomach, thighs, feet, and anywhere else he might be able to reach.
8) Realize that I've tossed the poopy pajamas onto the portable heater.
9) Remove the poopy pajamas from the portable heater before the smell of freshly baked number two fills the house.
10) Run and throw the pajamas into the washing machine and shut the lid. While there, take another big breath. Run back into Jack's room.
11) Turn Jack on his side and try to remove the poop-brick from his back. Try to use baby wipes, but it's too caked-on. I can't get a good grip on it.
12) Consider using my fingernails, but can't get myself to do it.
13) Look around and see a playing card on the carpet that Julia had been playing with.
14) Take the playing card and slide it in between the poop-brick and Jack's back.
15) Chisel poop-brick on all sides until I can pry it off it one giant piece.

16) Stare at giant poop-brick in awe before nearly throwing out my back picking it up and tossing in the diaper pail.
17) Take ten baby wipes out of the baby wipe box.
18) Hold Jack's legs with my left hand while I unfasten the diaper with my right hand to find an enormous pile of brown pudding where Jack's genitals used to be.
19) Realize that *this* poop is soft because his diaper acts like a Crock Pot.
20) Quickly clean Jack's genitals with all ten wipes, which I quickly throw away. The wipes, not Jack's genitals.
21) Put a clean diaper on him.
22) Wonder what the hell he's smiling about.
23) Wonder why I feel so faint before realizing I haven't taken a breath for the past two-and-a-half minutes.
24) Run out into the hallway to take another breath.
25) See Preva standing in the laundry room. She asks, "Did you just throw Jack's poopy jammies into the washing machine?"
26) I respond, "Yeah, why?"
27) "You just threw them onto an entire load of whites," she replies, holding Jack's jammies in one hand and a bunch of wet, white clothes in the other. "Now I have to wash the whole load again. Nice going."
28) "Sorry. But cut me some slack. I just changed the worst diaper in the world by myself, even though you're apparently awake and could have come helped," I say.
29) I don't actually say that. I just think it. All I actually say is "Sorry." But it's still on this list.

December 8, 2009
11:50 pm

I learned a new word today.

Thirty minutes ago, we were in the "El Pollo Loco" drive-thru, picking up lunch. "El Pollo Loco" is a fast-food place that serves pretty good chicken. In English, it means, "The place to go if you don't live near a Chick-Fil-A."

All four of us were in the car and we had just finished picking up our food. We started driving toward our house, with Preva's arm hanging out the window to try and cool off Julia's chicken poppers when her phone rang. It was her mom. For about a minute, they engaged in the usual mother-daughter chitchat. But then, Preva suddenly dropped the phone onto her lap and started laughing.

"What's going on?" I asked.

"Hang on, give me a second," she said as she continued laughing. She sighed and composed herself before turning to me and saying, "My mom wants to know what we're doing, because she's *bored*."

"Bored.... bored... " I muttered. "What does that word even mean?" I asked, unable to recall its definition. "I know what 'monotonous,' 'tired,' and 'worn out' mean. But 'bored'? Sorry. I'm drawing a blank."

"I think 'bored' is when you don't have anything to do," she replied.

"Oh yeah!" I said, a lightbulb going on in my head, as I realized that neither of us had been bored since the moment Julia had entered our lives and we certainly weren't bored now that Jack had joined us.

I quickly joined Preva in hysterics. Now I understood what was so funny.

"My mom's bored. Wants to know what we're doing," she deadpanned, as the humor grew in our frazzled, sleep-deprived heads.

"We have a newborn," I said. "What does she think we're doing? Hosting a dinner party for the governor?"

"What's a governor?" the nosiest three-year-old in the world wanted to know, as we continued laughing.

"*What the hell's going on*?!" I then heard my delicate flower of a wife's even more delicate flower of a mother screech into Preva's phone, which was still sitting in her lap.

"We're just laughing that you're bored," Preva explained.

"I'm a g.d. grandmother! I'm supposed to be bored!" she responded defensively, except that she didn't say, "g.d."

We couldn't argue with her logic and we certainly didn't begrudge her her boredom, especially since she helps with the kids. It was just the realization that some people look for ways to *fill* their days while we're simply struggling to *get through* ours struck us as incredibly funny at that moment.

We pulled up to a stoplight.

"My mom's bored!" Preva yelled out the window to no one in particular as she popped one of Julia's chicken poppers into her mouth. "Bored!"

The woman in the car next to us smiled as she rolled up her window, clearly wondering whether Preva had all of her marbles. She was right to wonder. I'm not sure that either of us has our marbles.

Wait. I remember what "bored" means. Now, what are "marbles" again?

Before we had kids.
Quite possibly the last time we were bored.

December 10, 2009
1:14 am

This just in… Sometimes too much beer is not so good.

December 10, 2009
10:55 pm

On Thursday mornings when I'm not working, I take Julia to gymnastics. I love watching Julia and the other three-year-olds do somersaults, touch their toes, and walk on the balance beam, which stands a death-defying six inches off the ground.

"Don't pick your nose, Cindy. It throws off your balance," Coach Chris says to one of the girls. Cindy doesn't stop picking, but she doesn't fall, either.

I also bring Jack with me, so that Preva has a chance to grab a morning nap. I enjoy bringing both kids to things like dance and gymnastics, because the other moms look at me like I'm SuperDad.

On more than one occasion, a mom has looked at me while I'm feeding Jack and said, "You're so good with him."

I'm not exactly sure what makes me "so good with him." Maybe it's that I don't hold him upside down by one foot when I feed him or that I place the bottle's nipple in his mouth rather than his ear.

I realize that what they're really saying is, "For a dad, you're so good with him." I'm okay with that, but it's a funny sort of a compliment. It's like being Japanese and having someone say, "You're a really good driver" or being Italian and having someone say, "You eat such sensible portions."

Today, I came to gymnastics with a new weapon in my SuperDad toolbelt: the ability to braid hair.

Our babysitter Stephanie is the resident hair expert, so the other day I had her give me a crash course in braiding. It wasn't easy, but with enough trial and "hair'er", I finally got the hang of it.

Although I'm usually late (and according to Preva, *always* late), I made sure to arrive to class ten minutes early. While the moms were chatting and Jack was napping in his stroller, I sat Julia on my lap and set to work.

As soon as I grabbed Julia's hairbrush and started brushing her hair, I felt the moms' heads turn almost in unison. I pretended not to notice, but I did. The pressure was on. I couldn't screw this up.

As they kept talking and I made small talk with Julia, I started dividing her hair into three sections and began braiding. I didn't want to go too fast and risk having the moms miss what I was doing. But I didn't want to go too slow and risk having Julia lose patience and squirm out of my lap. Premature lap-squirming is always a danger with Julia.

When I was about halfway done, I no longer heard the moms chatting. They were too busy watching SuperDad braid his daughter's hair. I started wishing that Stephanie had taught me how to "french braid" so that I could really blow their minds.

"Don't get cocky!" my inner-self warned as I placed a rubberband in my mouth. "You're not out of the woods yet!"

I then made a calculated but risky move. I turned toward the moms and smiled while I began trying her braids with the rubberband.

I was working blind and they knew it!

I then turned back toward Julia's braids and gave one final twist with the rubberband until it reached the appropriate tightness.

"All done," I casually said to Julia as I patted her tushy and she hopped off my lap.

"Thanks, daddy!" she chirped before giving me a quick kiss and running out onto the gymnastics mat with the other kids.

"Where did you learn how to braid hair?" one sufficiently impressed mom asked.

"I don't know," I responded. "It's just something I picked up."

"Wow," one mom said to another mom. "Can you imagine Jeff braiding hair?"

The other mom laughed and shook her head, clearly unable to imagine Jeff doing such a thing.

I was pleased. It couldn't have gone better. This would make a great story for years to come. Yet another one of those stories that would entertain our friends who have kids and bore the crap out of those who don't. But wait... even our friends with no kids might like it because of what happened next.

"Do you work?" another mom that I didn't recognize suddenly asked. She was new to the class.

"I work from home," I responded.

"Ahh," she said, smiling and nodding.

What the hell did that mean, I wondered? I had gone from being very proud to being incredibly annoyed. Did she not believe that I really had a job? Or was she one of those people who think that "working from home" means that you have a lame job where you just have to check your email every thirty minutes? I hate telling people that I work from home, because those are the two most common assumptions people make.

"Oh, *that's* why you to had time to learn how to braid," Annoying New Mom added.

"I actually have two jobs, but I'm a writer, so I'm able to work from home," I quickly explained.

My explanation fell on deaf ears, as Annoying New Mom was onto her next insulting question.

"Are you the dad?" she asked.

"Of course I'm the dad," I said, offended. "I'm here every week."

"Oh. We thought you were the uncle," said another mom who wasn't new and, until now, wasn't annoying.

Things had certainly taken a turn. I had very quickly gone from being SuperDad to an unemployed, possibly gay uncle who liked braiding hair.

I felt like my only shot at redemption was telling them that I only learned how to braid hair to try and wow them. My logic being that if feeding Jack without killing him amazed them, then braiding hair would blow their minds. But I didn't. I said nothing. I just watched the rest of class with Jack while the other moms talked about mom stuff amongst themselves.

I even changed a big poopy diaper while Jack was laying on my lap with no towel underneath and didn't get so much as a "way to go" head nod from any of the moms.

I probably deserved it. In the end, it wasn't a practical joke or performance art. It was just a waste of time. But at least I know how to braid hair.

December 11, 2009
8:44 am

Jack just laughed for the first time.

He was sitting in his electric swing wearing his favorite ensemble -- an Elmo t-shirt and a diaper. I was adjusting his diaper so that in the event that he peed, he wouldn't soak the swing.

As I pulled one side of the diaper down over his chubby little thighs, he started to giggle. I didn't even recognize the sound at first. I wasn't looking at his face, so I assumed it was the start of a crying fit or just a really high-pitched burp.

I then pulled the *other* side of diaper down over his *other* thigh and he made the same sound before I finally registered that it was laugh. My son was laughing!

I then did a funny face (or what I imagined a funny face might look like to a two-month old) and squeezed his thighs again. He laughed even louder. A feeling of warmth, pride, and for some reason, relief, passed over me unlike anything I'd ever experienced.

When quizzed by James Lipton, guests on Bravo's "Inside the Actor's Studio" always say that their favorite sound is their children's laughter, and I would have to agree.

I'd tried to make Jack laugh dozens of times before, but it never worked. He just wasn't ready. But today, for whatever reason, he finally decided it was time.

Neither Preva nor Julia was there. It was just me. A special moment between father and son I'll never forget.

December 12, 2009
11:34 pm

Tonight, Preva's parents were kind enough to take the kids for a couple of hours so that we could have a date night. For two exhausted parents who have yet to do any Christmas shopping, a Friday "date night" equals "trip to Costco." The full extent of just how sad that is still hasn't hit me yet and I hope it never does.

We were returning a fake Christmas tree, which was six inches too tall for our living room. I hate returning things to the store. However, my Jewish wife had her heart set on getting the perfect Christmas tree, and this one didn't fit the bill.

We arrived at Costco at around 6:30, where we found a good news/bad news situation. The bad news was that it was so crowded, whenever I stopped for a food sample and tried to put it in my mouth, I would accidentally feed the guy next to me. The good news is that out of our valley of 300,000 people, approximately 12 people weren't there, so it wasn't as packed as it could have been.

After we returned our tree, we tried to find a shorter one, but naturally, they were out. We shifted our focus to gift buying. However, we were too tired to fight the crowds or stand in the long checkout lines, so we opted for a romantic dinner instead.

We'd planned on going out for sushi, but we were both starving, so we made the logical choice. We walked up to the Costco food counter.

"May I help you," the typically polite Costco employee asked.

"Yes," I replied. "The lady will have the baked chicken wrap and I will have the turkey wrap and a slice of pizza."

I then asked to see the wine list. Preva punched me in the arm as I was told, "We only have Coke and stuff like that."

I was about to go back to the impressive Costco wine section, but buying a bottle there would require braving the aforementioned checkout lines. I then remembered that I had a really nice bottle in my car that I received at "America's Funniest Videos" as a Christmas present. While Preva waited on the food, I went and got it.

The only open table we found was in the back near the bathrooms. With our ten dollar meal and our eighty dollar bottle of wine, we commenced dining.

I'm not sure what was more entertaining: watching families trying to survive holiday shopping at Costco without killing each other or "getting our drink on" and not letting anyone see us swigging Merlot straight from the bottle.

When you don't have you kids with you, it's fun to laugh at people who do. It's even more fun with wine.

Not wanting to let the endlessly entertaining parade of holiday shoppers go to waste, we decided to have our own private awards show called "The Costies." We were both the hosts and the audience as we handed out awards for every category we could think of:

"Couple Most Likely to Divorce Before Christmas"
"Mom Most In Need of a Caribbean Vacation All By Herself"
"Dad Most Likely to Threaten Another Dad with a Giant Jar of Mayonnaise"
"Kid Least In Need of Two Giant Slices of Cheese Pizza"
"Couple Most Likely to Accidentally Leave Their Kid at Costco"
"Couple Most Likely to Intentionally Leave Their Kid at Costco"

We didn't actually walk over and give them awards, but we did eat cheap food and drink expensive Merlot in their honor.

There's no better place to enjoy the fun, craziness, and temporary moments of insanity experienced by the typical family than at a Costco right before Christmas. We spent more than an hour laughing at everything that everyone was going through.

We finished our food and then waited long enough for me to sober up enough to drive home where we quickly resumed being the kind of family that we'd spent the night making fun of.

December 13, 2009
10:50 pm

About thirty minutes ago, Jack fell asleep while I was holding him. I laid him down on the bed, expecting him to wake up ten or fifteen minutes later, but he didn't. Pretty soon it was twenty minutes and then thirty minutes. He never "naps" at night for that long.

So, I just did something I'll probably regret. I just went and laid him down in his crib. I don't want him to wake up screaming, waking both Julia and Preva, who really needs her sleep. I'll conk out about two minutes from now, so I have to make sure I get him the instant he starts crying.

December 14, 2009
8:18 am

I woke up at 6:51 am. But Jack was still asleep!

I never heard him cry last night after I put him to bed. I figured that I was just sleeping too soundly and that Preva must have heard him and gotten him.

I found her downstairs making pancakes. I asked her about it, but she said that she never went into his room!

ME: "Good morning."
PREVA: "Good morning, honey."
ME: "What time did you have to get Jack?"
PREVA: "I didn't."
ME: "What do you mean?"
PREVA: "I never went into his room."
ME: "You must have."
PREVA: "I didn't."
ME: "Somebody did."
PREVA: "Like who? Julia? You think she made him a bottle, put him in the Bjorn until he fell asleep, and then stuck him in his crib?"
ME: "Are you messing with me?"
PREVA: "Are you messing with *me*?"

ME: "I put him in bed around 10:20 last night. There's no way he slept all the way through the night. There's no way he's still sleeping!"

Preva broke into a huge smile. I stared at her for a second before I bolted upstairs to grab the baby monitor. I turned it on and saw Jack sleeping like, well, a baby.

Preva walked in and saw me holding the monitor. I handed it to her and collapsed on the bed in a mild state of shock. She lay down next to me.

"Maybe this is it!" I said, beaming. "Maybe that's the end of it!"

"Let's not get too excited," she responded. "Let's just look at it as one good night. At the very least, he's starting to turn the corner."

"Yeah, but people say that it ends just like that," I repeated, no doubt sounding ungrateful for the first eight straight hours of sleep I've had since Jack was born.

"You better knock on wood, Lohla!" Preva said.

I nodded before leaning over and giving our headboard a good hard whack. I then scooted closer to it, running my hand along its smooth wooden surface.

"What are you doing?" Preva asked.

"It's been so long since any part of either of our bodies came anywhere close to knocking into that headboard, I forgot it was even there," I answered.

She laughed and rolled on top of me, giving me a look I hadn't seen in way too long.

"What about your pancakes?" I asked.

"The pancakes can wait," she said, as I held her face and pulled her to me.

It's truly amazing what a good night's sleep can do.

December 14, 2009
2:11 pm

Jack woke up at 7:12 a.m today. He slept nearly nine hours last night. Unbelievable! That's four hours longer than the previous record!

For the most part, he seems like the same kid. But there's something different about him. I don't mean that his hair has changed color or that his circumcision has reversed itself.

But something has changed. It's hard to explain. He just seems slightly more "at peace" somehow. He's not as whiny and when he does cry, he doesn't do it with quite the same fury as he did just yesterday.

I don't know if the new and improved Jack has arrived, but I sure hope he has. I'm really hoping for Jack 3-point-oh. (Jack 2-point-oh was the version that Apple rushed to market too quickly, causing Steve Jobs to make the person responsible for it "conveniently disappear.")

Trying to enjoy the "wild ride."
(I'm not above the occasional "hit you over the head" metaphor every now and then.)

December 14, 2009
11:15 pm

It's 11:15. I put Jack in bed an hour ago and so far, so good. It's the second consecutive night that I've put him down before 10:30. I'm too nervous that he'll wake up and too excited that he's asleep to actually fall asleep myself.

Right before I put him down, I was watching a show featuring the Sextomom from the "mom with too many kids" show that I saw several weeks ago. The one who had the balls to tell me, "Don't wish it away."

Well, I'm here to say that tonight she redeemed herself with one more bit of advice. The advice was, "This too shall pass."

I like "This too shall pass." I would have a beer with "This too shall pass." Because "This too shall pass" acknowledges how hard it is having kids and actually gives comfort, whereas "Don't wish it away" makes good parents feel guilty if they can't help longing for the better days and nights that lie ahead.

I didn't think that Sextomom could have even more mottos than she has kids, but apparently she does.

I don't know if Jack's colic is about to be a thing of the past. But I do find solace in the fact that the worst of it is now behind us.

December 15, 2009
7:33 am

I woke up an hour ago and turned on the baby monitor. Jack was still asleep. That's two nights in a row!

I leaned over and kissed Preva. I then spooned Snort and Preva spooned Bentley and all four of us fell back asleep with big grins on our well-rested faces.

I really shouldn't say this, and I realize that I'm probably just jinxing us, but it looks like Jack's colic is no more. &$*#)@)($*#* yes!

December 16, 2009
11:11 am

See ya, colic. It was horrible knowing you.

Last night was the third night in a row that Jack slept more than eight straight hours. His previous record was nearly five, which was only achieved once or twice.

Not only is he sleeping longer, but when he cries, it's not like it used to be. He doesn't clench his fists. His face doesn't get red. Overall, it's like he's a different kid. It's very strange. An awesome kind of strange.

Life is good again. It's amazing how much better everything is when you get enough sleep. Colors are brighter. Showers are more invigorating. People picking their noses in the cars next to me don't annoy or disgust me as much. I've even had time to resume eating and blinking.

Jack's colic wasn't caused by gas or stomach discomfort or abdominal pain or allergies or neurological overload or not holding him enough or not making enough "whooshing" or "shushing" sounds to simulate what it was like in the womb or anything else that we'd read or heard could cause it.

He simply wasn't ready for the world yet. It's been said that some babies just need a "fourth trimester" to adjust to, and feel comfortable in, their new surroundings. That's the only thing that makes sense.

We didn't do anything differently the day before Jack's colic ended than we did the day that it finally ended. He was ready when he was ready and there was nothing we could do to make that happen any faster.

Jack just needed time. It's as simple as that. Or maybe he just wanted me to write a book about him and this is the only thing he could come up with.

Well, my son, it worked. Now everybody knows about your comically small penis. How'd that work out for you?

December 19, 2009
4:41 pm

Last night was a night that we'd been looking forward to for a long time. It was the annual Mark and Brian Christmas Show, which always features plenty of great bands and A-list comedians.

However, we were mostly looking forward to hanging out with Mark and Brian and all the show's other "family members," whom we hadn't seen since Preva was in the hospital. Preva's mom was watching the kids for what was supposed to be a fun "date night"-slash-"end of colic celebration," since Jack had slept through the night the previous five nights.

Unfortunately, an hour before we were supposed to leave, we noticed that Jack's forehead was hot. But it wasn't just his forehead. His entire body was on fire. He was also more irritable than usual. We quickly took his temperature, which was 103.

We called our doctor, who said that we should immediately take him to urgent care. It could just be a fever, he said, but since Jack's too young to be fully vaccinated, we needed to rule out the more serious possibilities that can be fatal to a baby.

Preva's mom kindly offered to take him for us, but we declined, feeling that we needed to be there. And just like that, it was goodbye "date night," hello "worst night of screaming yet."

We brought Jack in and the fifty-something male nurse asked all the usual questions and took all the usual measurements. Then it was time to draw blood. We thought that after what we've been through the past couple of months, we could handle what was about to happen. Turns out, we couldn't.

First, he tried an i.v. in Jack's arm, while Preva and I tried to soothe him. But Jack's what they call "big-boned," so his copious flab made it impossible.

After trying in vain for ten minutes to try and find a vein, the nurse finally just stuck the needle in. To no one's surprise, the attempt failed and Jack wailed. He tried again. Same result.

Preva asked, "Do we really have to do this?!"

"He'll be okay," I said, squeezing her hand.

Then the nurse moved to Jack's hand -- the *back* of Jack's hand. They massaged and manipulated for another ten minutes trying to find a vein and get the angle of the prick just right, all the while Jack's crying is an "11" on a scale of 1 to 10. Then he stuck it in.

Jack cried so hard, his body shook. His face turned purple. His screaming was so loud and so high-pitched, it sounded like a car alarm fighting with a dog whistle. Preva couldn't bear to look.

And yet, there was still no blood entering the syringe. The nurse tried again. He was out of breath and sweating.

The combination of Jack's tears and the nurse's sweat soaked the protective paper covering the examining table.

"Don't worry," the nurse said. "I've done this for twenty years and never failed to draw blood from a baby."

After that, he moved to Jack's leg, where he promptly failed to draw blood from a baby for the first time in twenty years. Jack finally had a legitimate reason to cry and he was making the most of it.

Why now? We just started to like him.

He then said he'd need to prick Jack's heel, which he said was an effective, but painful last resort.

"We can't keep doing this to him!" Preva said, her voice trembling.

I told the nurse he would need to have the doctor help him for this last part, because we couldn't handle seeing Jack in any more agony.

We walked to the end of the hallway and locked ourselves in the bathroom. We turned on the fan, crouched down in the corner, covered our ears, and held our breath.

"Are we terrible parents?" Preva asked.

"Maybe. But he's a terrible baby," I reasoned.

She put her head on my shoulder and whispered, "He *used* to be a terrible baby. I can't believe how much I love him."

Seconds later, we heard a loud, scary, unmistakably Jack-like scream. It continued for another five minutes until finally, it was quiet.

We quickly hustled down the hallway to find a son that was out of tears and a vial that was full of blood.

At long last, it was over. We quickly dressed Jack and gave him some Tylenol before putting him in the car and driving home. I wasn't sure who had been through more that night: Jack, Preva, or the Amazing Sweaty Male Nurse of Valencia.

Jack woke up once around three, but after we gave him a bottle and some Tylenol, he quickly fell back sleep.

When we got the results of the blood work, we were relieved to hear that it was just a standard fever. He'd probably caught something from his sister who'd probably caught something from someone in her preschool.

Today, he's napped more than usual and been understandably fussy from all the pokes and pricks all over his body. We're just glad he's okay.

His colic might be over, but we're starting to get the feeling that he's always going to make things interesting.

December 20, 2009
2:05 pm

Jack still has a slight fever, but he's feeling and looking much better today. The life has returned to his eyes and the volume has returned to his crying

We were afraid Jack's illness would reawaken his colic and bring Jackula back from the dead, but fortunately, it didn't. He slept through the night yet again. His colic is finally and unmistakably gone.

Preva just came downstairs and asked me a question that we'd both considered, yet never actually discussed (probably because we were both afraid of the answer). She asked, "If Jack was our first baby, do you think we'd have another?"

I thought for a minute before giving her a firm and unequivocal, "Maybe."

"If you'd asked me a month ago, I would have said 'No way'," she responded.

"But now you're a 'maybe'?" I asked.

"I'm more like an 'I wouldn't rule it out'," she said.

I said, "If you're already an 'I wouldn't rule it out,' then by next week, you'll be an 'Of course I would'."

Preva smiled. "Go empty the diaper pail. It stinks."

December 26, 2009
4:15 pm

Jack turned three months old today.

We're in San Diego celebrating Christmas at my parents' house. We had a great Christmas Eve and an even better Christmas Day, primarily because Jack slept from 9 p.m. to 7 a.m. both nights.

Jack's colic is no more. And just like the "Texas Hold 'Em" poker craze, it pretty much ended "just like that."

I went into this thinking that I might discover what "caused" Jack's colic or what would somehow "cure" it, but I didn't. I still have no idea. And nobody else can tell me that they do, either. I'll admit that there might be different *types* of colic, but with Jack's type, the only cure was time.

But it's not really about a cure. It's about survival. What's important is maintaining your sanity by sleeping every spare minute you can, finding some way to laugh in the midst of the craziness, and looking for support wherever you can find it. You need to realize that you're not alone and that it will eventually get better. It's absolutely essential for both you and your baby.

Because crazy thoughts can race through your mind at three a.m. when your baby is screaming and you're so exhausted you can barely think. You can't control the crying. The only thing you can control is your reaction when you realize that you can't stop the crying.

In all, Jack's colic lasted a little more than eleven weeks. Eleven weeks doesn't sound like that long. But when each one of those days is the longest day of your life, it adds up pretty fast.

Some babies stay colicky for a lot longer, so we realize it could have been so much worse. Then again, it could have been so much better.

We never took for granted how lucky we are to have a healthy baby boy. But we'll also never forget just how difficult and psychologically taxing this was.

We had a few laughs and more than a few cries. The cries will be easier to remember than the laughs, so I'm glad I kept this "diary" to help me remember.

I love my son, I love my family, and I love feeling like a real person again. I wouldn't wish having a baby with colic on anyone. But I also don't regret wishing it away.

Because even back then, I knew that very soon I would get to a point where I would never wish away another second.

That's my son. That's my Jack.

ACKNOWLEDGMENTS

I would like to thank the following people for helping make this book possible.

Preva… For being my amazing wife and best friend and for giving me two (can't believe you went through the whole ordeal *twice*!) amazing kids.

Julia… For being the coolest, sweetest daughter on earth and making me want another child.

Jack… For (finally) turning into the son I always wanted.

Jerry and Roberta Lohla (Gigi and Papa)… For being the best parents a guy could have and for fostering an unhealthy love of UNC basketball and the Atlanta Braves (Papa only).

Roy and Susan Fleischman (Grandma and Grandpa)… For being amazing in-laws and raising a daughter who is everything I was looking for and could have asked for.

Dr. Vadapalli and Dr. Yen… For being the best pediatricians in Santa Clarita. Thank you Dr. Yen for keeping Jack out of the NICU!
www.santaclaritapediatrics.com

Entéra – the Artist… For the "devil in a diaper" front cover illustration.
www.entera-theartist.com

Susan Updegraft… For the picture on the back cover. capturetheessence@att.net

Seth Jaret… For being a terrific manager. Check out Content Engine. (www.contentengine.tv)

Matt Grenewetzki… For designing the website.

Brian Phelps… For being so funny and supportive.

Mark Thompson… For being so supportive and old.

Vin Di Bona… For creating an awesome show that I'm proud to work on.

Todd Thicke… For being a great boss and for the fact that one time when he was asked if he'd like lobster for dinner, he replied, "No, I ate lobster all weekend."

Jack and Julia's cousins Jake, Kyle, and Alex… For nothing in particular. But it's cool being in a book, isn't it?

Chris, Ande, and Kenzie… For just being you.

Larry and Sheri Fleischman… For giving us enough love to fill a storage unit.
www.extraspace.com

Gary Choppé… For designing the book cover.
www.choppeadvertisinggroup.com

Svetlana Busse… For keeping Preva "calm" during both of her deliveries. The most awesome nurse in Awesometown.

Stephanie Basey… For being the best, most upbeat nannysitter in the world.

Bentley and Snort… For always licking our faces when we needed it most.

Delta Airlines… For stopping the plane.

• • • • •

Just a few more thank you's to some of you who have supported, inspired, entertained, befriended, or simply been related to me over the years (though many of you ended up supporting and/or inspiring and/or doing something to make me want to mention you, too). And I'm certain that I would have included you even if email and social networking sites like Facebook didn't exist for you to tell your friends and family about this book and how cool it is that your name is in it, hint-hint, nudge-nudge, wink-wink…

Grandma Julia, Papa Jack, "America's Funniest Home Videos", www.facebook.com/AFV, Michele Nasraway, Marybeth Thicke, The Palleschis: Mike (he has a leather jacket), Yanti, Max, and Jellie, alexandriahouse.org, Tom Bergeron, Jordan and Ellie Schatz, Nicolas Cage, Tomika Palmer, Jess Harnell, Brad Gage, Chad Goldich, E.C. Pauling, Vin Diesel, Matt Woolsey, Rich Connor, Ashley Cicconi, Moira Keihm, Brian, Karin, and Hannah Hudson, ww5.komen.org, Jim Morris (he of the writing, yoga, and walking his dog) and Melissa Lauer, Ethan and Lisa Berghoff (Yeti and wife), Sanjib and Kathy Mohanty, Charles Dickens, Bobby Cox (thanks for all you did for the Braves and for retiring), Brent Guttman (for his financial "advice"), Pete Geraci, Luke Geraci, Pete (Big Pete) and

Carol Geraci, Miller Lite, Dick and Judy Robison, Russell and Doracy Harrison, Matt and Heather Robison, Dateline's Keith Morrison, The Kinks, David Byers, Greg Erb, Jeff and Robin Schultz, Animal Specialty Group and everyone who helped Bentley live eleven months longer than she would have (Dr. Mary Kay Blake, Jenella, Aleta, Velvet, Dr. Becker, Dr. Bonaparte, Caty, and Layne) Dr. Amber Wheelbarger, Kevin "Two Soups" Kataoka, Gabby, Michael, Aine, Connor, and Morgan Taylor, Rita Wilde, Ginger Jones, Dr. Jim Sears from "The Doctors", whoever greenlighted the film "Point Break", Carrie, Pierce, and John "Batman" McAdam, www.thepilatespros.com (the best pilates studio in Valencia), Henry Miller, Kurt Vonnegut, Lewis Grizzard, Dave Barry, Rick Reilly, Michael and Kirsten Nielsen (best composer/t-ball coach and team mom in Valencia), www.thesweetswiper.com (the best baking blog), Buddy and Abigail Harris, Dan and Natalie Dunn, Jillian Reynolds of "Good Day L.A." for her great work with animals (and she shares Jack's b'day!), Ryan and Bethany Wanamaker, Zelma Phelps (Brian's sweet, awesome mom), Stacey Walkes, Josh Weiss, Italy, Rich, Missy, Michael, and Paulina Vokulich, Susan's friend Irene, Uncle Sandy and Aunt Shirley Walkes, Franny "Bobanny Sarge" Spitzer, Tom Hanks (thanks for letting Preva go to Mark and Brian to meet me), Dean Smith, "Cupcake Wars" (that's from my wife and daughter), hassle-free banking, Scott Gibson, Mr. Floppy, Steve Martin, Tania and Matt Gouvion, Rachel Weil of www.baileygivesback.org for her inspiring work with animals, Dennis and Susan McGarry, whatever ad agency thought to call Valencia, CA "Awesometown" to try and make it sound cooler, Brandon and Teri Zimon, Larry King, Heather and Max Subin, Joel and Ethan Coen, Twizzlers, anyone who saves a life by getting a pet from a shelter instead of a breeder, The Paseo Club, Fran Dubner (the best teacher at Dunwoody High), Karma Rescue www.karmarescue.org, Michael Roth, "The Onion," Larry Gilbert, Jim Mingin, "Airplane!", Jason and Nicole Sperling, Fatheads, Mike Karanovich, Alex Shaw, Harvey Altman and Company, Robert Urio, Philip Rackin, Marion Cotillard, Lynda Thompson (for catching what I hope were the last three "typos" in the book, but almost certainly weren't), Matt Thompson, Amy Thompson (Mark's aforementioned colicky baby!), Katie Thompson, movies where a guy asks a girl out and she says, "I'd like that," Marion Cotillard (I really like Marion Cotillard), Adam Geraci (you know what you did), Blake McCormick (you don't know what you did), Olivia Geraci, Ken and Anna Geraci, Dr. Brynie Collins (the best pediatric gastroenterologist in L.A.!), "30 Rock", palm trees, Alan Segal (the tallest, blondest Jewish guy in Dunwoody), Wolton and Soojoon Choi, Tostitos Restaurant Style with a Hint of Lime tortilla chips, Tina Fey, the soft drink "Wink" (loved that stuff) Steve, Dakota, Hunter, and Veronica Smith, http://muybuenocookbook.wordpress.com, John and Alicia Bowers, the show "Ugly Americans", Garrett and Jaemie Colley (I hear you have a lot of Facebook friends), Chris and Max Young (I hear you do, too), Todd Donoho, Tyler Hansbrough, The Simpsons, teachers, Julie, Joel, Kaden, and Kory Bystrom, Albany, Georgia, Allyson Arons, Krysti Carrelli, www.nothingbutnets.net, Donnie Osmond, Kristen Le Falle, The Siegels, The Zimrings, The Brodies, www.brodieelectric.com, Elizabeth Buraglio, "Spinal Tap", Aunt Mary Walkes, sleep, wharfs, when people in movies introduce other people to their "associates", Thad Brown, Oprah, Uncle Murray and Aunt Dolly, girls who think, "You know what? I'd like to wear a shirt that exposes my midriff, but I probably shouldn't," The Mungers, Kim Goldman, www.helpnothassle.org, Funyuns, E. Paul Edwards, blackjack, monkeys, the fact that whenever someone forgets my name they tend to call me "Chris" because I evidently look like a "Chris", Alicia, Susan Downey, Mel and Sue French, Steve Jolly, Phoebe Cates, Matt Bedrosian, The Santa Barbara Zoo, Sandra Lollino of www.flff.org, our cats B.G. and Pele, Erick Weber of NECN, Carter Johnson, Roy Williams (two titles at UNC in his first six years!) Hubert Davis, Antawn Jamison, Ed Cota, Jeff Lebo, Serge Zwikker, Pete Chilcutt, Harrison Barnes, Ed Geth, Scott May, Scott Cherry, Raymond Felton, Sam Perkins, Jimmy Black, Mike O'Koren, Mitch Kupchak, Tyler Zeller, Ranzino Smith, Cecil Exum, Adam Lucas (nice reporting), real estate infomercials, Phineas and Ferb, gold, our peeps at Sunshine Learning Center – Kara, Keelan, Lacey, Sandy, Mindy, Wendy, and Grant, Sandy Doerr (a million thanks!), "Weird Al" Yankovic, Dale Murphy, John Smoltz, Captain Over, Dewey Cox, Ron Burgundy, Nathan Arizona, Ken Burns' "Baseball", Bess Walkes, www.curesearch.org, when people say "graphic novel" instead of "comic book" because it sounds cooler, Mike and Judy Golub (thanks for "Ellie"!!!), Michael, Janet, and Sasha Leitman, John Latham, "The Kid Stays in the Picture," Adam Reicheg, Jennifer Reicheg, Marlene Reicheg, The Cat Doctor and Friends in Santa Clarita (Dr. Tracy McFarland, Dr. Rebecca Palmer), Scooby-Doo, Jessica Boothe, Dan Piraro's "Bizarro", Kiwi Smith, more bang for your buck, Dominique Wilkins, hand sanitizer, "Curb Your Enthusiasm", Matt and Joanna Johnson, Paulina Porizkova, Kristen Wiig, The Goldbergs, "Modern Family", Carl Kennedy, Jerry Seinfeld, Rick and Pat Kessler, www.shanesinspiration.com, The Ronald McDonald House, Elizabeth Kessler, Shooting Stars Center in Stevenson Ranch -- www.shootingstarscenter.com, Steve and Lee Laddy, Mike, Deb, Chantelle, and Jenna Delisser (Canadians!), Kathy Conte, Mrs. Henry and the amazing staff at "West Creek Academy" in Valencia, Sue and Mike

LaRaus, the Howard Walkes family, Kim and Kim at "Bake Me Happy" in Valencia, Larry and Carol Gold, Sir Dr. Stephen T. Colbert D.F.A., Aalok and Sejal Kuthiala, Robert and Ruby Straley, Roxanne Stralcy, Ron Stralcy, Steve and Amy Straley, Jaimie Straley, Luke Perry, low-cal margarita mix, the Leunis Family, seafood, Scott Mactavish ("The New Dad's Survival Guide"), Marion Cotillard again, the crew at KLOS 95.5: Bob, Carrie, and Pippen Buchmann, Daniel, Rebecca and Kobe Mizrahi, Mike and Jamie Sherry, Ted Lekas and Sue Funkhouser, Frank and Erin Sontag, Kelli Gates, Bob Moore, Craig Rossi, Vernon, Leonard, Spence, Arlene, Skylord, Sammi, Evelina, Roxanne, Rhonda, Mary, Officer (Q-Dog) Quarterman, Mike Olson, Bill Huning, Tito Benavides, Ernesto de la O, Joe and Elizabeth McDonnell, Gary Moore, Cynthia Fox, Lorie Carter, David O'Brien of Frontier Toyota, Garry Marshall, Trevor Astbury, Art and Kelli Altounian, The Beatles, and David Letterman.

10585109R10100

Made in the USA
Charleston, SC
17 December 2011